AT WATER'S EDGE

Also by Roger Bansemer:

The Art of Hot-Air Ballooning
Southern Shores
Rachael's Splendifilous Adventure

AT WATER'S EDGE
The Birds of Florida

Roger Bansemer
with
Bill Renc

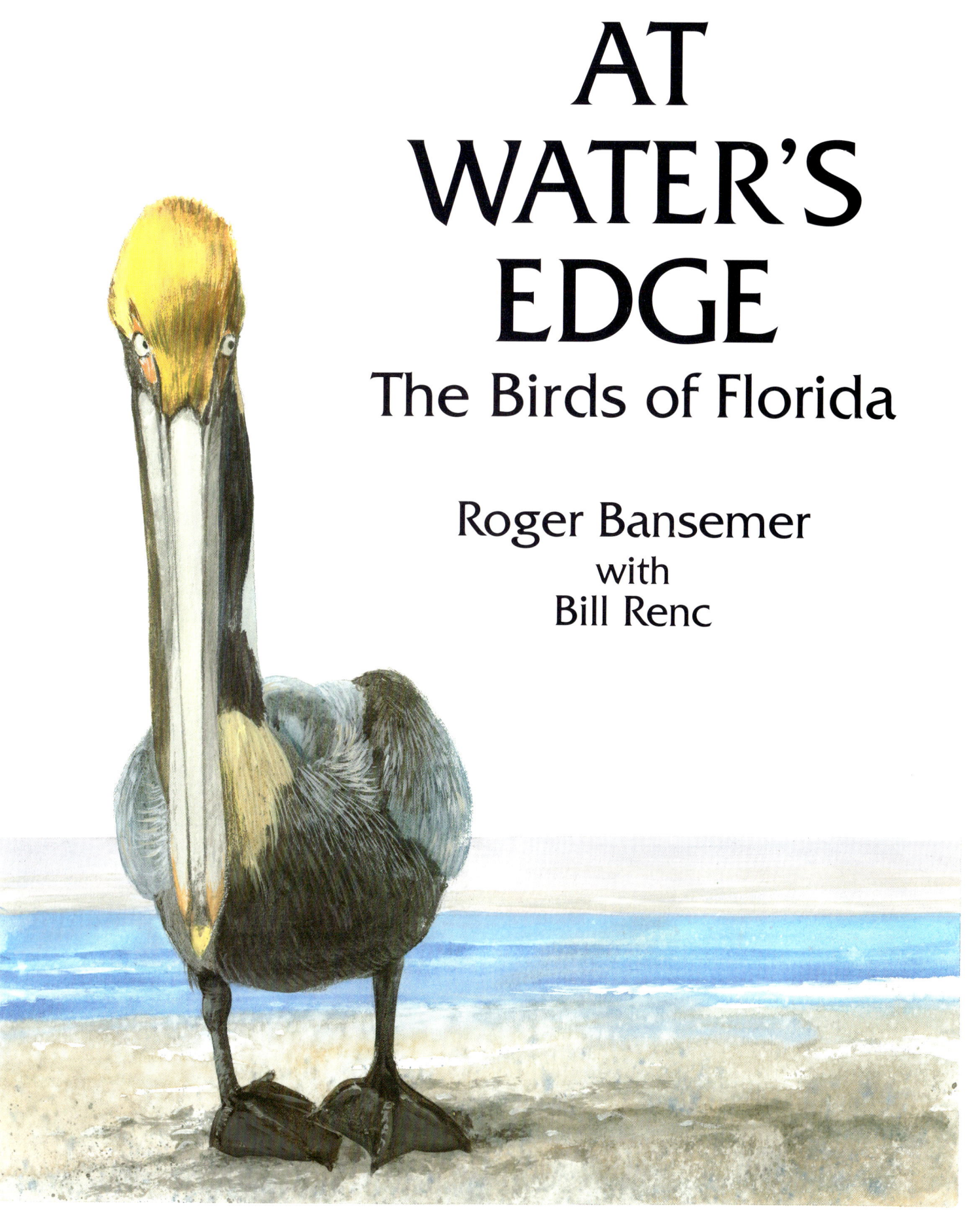

Paintings with thin white border are by Roger Bansemer.
Other paintings by Bill Renc.
Text by Roger Bansemer and Bill Renc

Calligraphy by Linda Renc

Thanks to:
Ernie Simmons
Bonnie Hite

Copyright ©1993 by Roger Bansemer and Bill Renc

All rights reserved.

No part of this book may be reproduced in any form without written permission from the publisher.

Published by Taylor Publishing Company
1550 West Mockingbird Lane
Dallas, Texas 75235

Library of Congress Cataloging-in-Publication Data

Bansemer, Roger.
    At water's edge : the birds of Florida / Roger Bansemer with Bill Renc.
      p. cm.
    ISBN 0-87833-821-7
    1. Birds—Florida.   I. Renc, Bill. II. Title
QL684.F6B35   1993
598.29759—dc20   92-37447
                                                                     CIP

Printed in the United States of America
10 9 8 7 6 5 4 3 2 1

*For our daughters
Lauren and Rachael Bansemer
and
Christine Renc*

Introduction

When I first came to Florida as a small boy, several things fascinated me. There was the thought of finding alligators around each corner—and we occasionally saw one where I lived. The shops along the beach at that time were full of straw-stuffed caymans, which looked just like alligators. I had to have one. They usually sat alongside shell lamps with bright pink plastic Flamingos plastered into the base. Other memories include seeing my first Dolphin and thinking it was a shark in the water as I raced in from the surf. More gentle memories were of the many large and exotic birds that casually flew into our backyard. They were looking for insects or fish from our lake or more often for a free hot dog or crust of bread from the family. They became friends and we waited for their arrival at about the same time every day, usually around dusk. A routine handout to a Great Egret named Elmer was my father's dedicated assignment to himself. Since then I have been a casual bird watcher and as an artist have been fascinated by their motion and shapes against the unequalled beauty of Florida's cloud-filled skies.

Since those early days of my childhood, where I grew up, the landscape of the Florida shores has been transformed from miles of untouched mangrove forests into a skyline of high-rise buildings. The wildlife habitat has more or less been forgotten in these areas. The sand has been replaced with concrete and where nesting birds once raised their young, manicured lawns completely devoid of natural habitat prevail. Some of the animals have adapted quite well, but others have not. Terns find nesting on the large flat gravel roofs of industrial buildings and shopping centers quite satisfactory while others, like the Skimmers who have given this a try, have met with little success.

With the invention of the jet ski and the increase of recreational boating, nesting sights on the shores of small islands are constantly being disrupted for the sake of entertainment. Birds that leave their nests when frightened also leave eggs exposed to the hot Florida sun, which can soon kill them. Sea grasses are uprooted, leaving bays scarred by the trails of motorboats.

In the last century, hunters almost eradicated many of Florida's birds. Today the situation is different, but the impact on the bird community is the same. The replacement of natural habitat to suit our current tastes in landscape leaves many areas along our coast devoid of places for birds to live as well as many other forms of sealife that get their start in the shallows. Sensitivity towards what nature has provided needs to be considered more than it has been when it comes to development. Mangroves, palmettos and numerous other native plants help support wildlife and need to be left undisturbed in the urban landscape rather than replaced with cultivated plants. Incorporating them into our scheme of things during development is indispensable if we wish to keep intact the things we came to Florida for in the first place. The food chain of the wildlife around us is dependent on this habitat and sooner or later it affects us directly. If mangroves disappear, the spawning areas of fish disappear, then the birds leave, and before you know it there are no longer fish for either humans or birds, and the system starts to break down in all directions. If birds have disappeared from your area, most likely the habitat on which they rely has been disrupted and their food supply cut off. They move on and their numbers diminish.

Birds are good indicators of things to come that may affect us later on. The DDT used in the 1960's almost eliminated the population of Brown Pelicans in Florida and in fact did eliminate them in Louisiana. It caused the eggshells to be thin, and as a result they were broken before the young hatched. When the chemical was banned, pelicans and birds of prey started to make a comeback. It is hard to believe that this chemical along with many others has not affected us in ways we may not even know about. Pelicans had to be reintroduced to Louisiana and now are making a good comeback. Even though Pelicans seem common here today, it has been only a few years since they were taken off the endangered list.

The biggest threat to our Florida birds is man. Monofilament fishing line alone kills dozens of Pelicans every year by entangling them. Fishing hooks kill dozens more. Litter does the same thing to birds that get entangled or swallow plastic trash floating in the water. There are a number of wildlife rehabilitation centers around the state, and if you find an injured bird, the Game and Freshwater Fish Commission can give you information where such places are. The Suncoast Seabird Sanctuary located in Redington Shores near St. Petersburg is one such place. It is the largest in the state and each year they treat over 7,000 birds. Amazingly, 85 to 90 percent of the bird injuries are man-related.

The birds of Florida are truly worthy of our admiration. Our book takes you on a tour of what is certainly an irreplaceable asset to our state and we hope will give you more understanding of these special animals.

Our book is not meant to tell you everything that is known about these birds. In fact, the lives of many remain mysterious to even the most knowledgeable bird watcher and are full of contradictions. Bill Renc and I have instead tried to depict in an artistic way the majesty and wonderment of these treasures at water's edge.

Contents

Anhinga	10	Green-backed Heron		Curlew	
Cormorant	12	Wurdemann's Heron		Whimbrel	
Double-crested Cormorant		American Bittern		Marbled Godwit	
Coots, Galinules, Moorhens	14	*Ibis*	58	Black-bellied Plover	
Clapper Rail	16	White Ibis		Ruddy Turnstone	
Loon	17	Glossy Ibis		Red Knot	
Common Loon		*Habitats*	69	Least Sandpiper	
Eagle	18	Mangroves		Sanderling	
Bald Eagle		Ocean Beaches		Semipalmated Sandpiper	
Egrets	20	Marshlands		Dunlin	
Great Egret		Open Ocean		Size Comparison of Shorebirds	
Cattle Egret		Estuaries		*Skimmer*	110
Reddish Egret		Cypress Swamps		Black Skimmer	
Snowy Egret		Rivers and Lakes		*Spoonbill*	114
Flamingo	30	Prairies		Roseate Spoonbill	
Frigatebird	32	*Kingfisher*	78	*Stork*	118
Magnificent Frigatebird		Belted Kingfisher		Wood Stork	
Gulls	34	*Limpkin*	80	*Terns*	120
Herring Gull		*Osprey*	82	Royal Tern	
Laughing Gull		*Oystercatcher*	84	Common Tern	
Ring-billed Gull		American Oystercatcher		Forster's Tern	
Herons	38	*Pelicans*	86	Sandwich Tern	
Great Blue Heron		Brown Pelican		Noddy Tern	
Tricolored Heron		White Pelican		Sooty Tern	
Little Blue Heron		*Sandhill Crane*	94	Least Tern	
Great White Heron		*Shorebirds*	98	*Vultures*	126
Yellow Crowned Night Heron		Dowitcher		Turkey Vulture	
Black Crowned Night Heron		Black-necked Stilt		Black Vulture	
		Willet			
		Yellowlegs			

Anhinga

Looking as if it is made of polished ebony, the statuesque Anhinga perches with its wings spread and head in a noble profile as though posing for an artist. However, this is not an invitation to get close. They are shy birds and quickly fly away or disappear under water if approached.

When it dives for fish, the feathers of the Anhinga become saturated with water. Unlike most birds, their feathers lack oil glands and are not waterproof, allowing the bird to submerge easily. They are quite capable of flying when totally drenched, but regularly dry themselves in the sun and breeze before taking flight. This characteristic is also true of the Cormorant.

Using its large webbed feet for torpedolike speed and its sharp pointed bill to spear fish broadside, the Anhinga is an expert underwater fisherman. When surfacing with its catch, the Anhinga shakes its head to loosen the prey before swallowing it head first.

Unlike the Cormorant's hooked bill, the Anhinga's bill is sharply pointed. The Anhinga's body is also longer and more slender. When young, both the Cormorant and Anhinga breathe through their nostrils, but soon the bone structure grows together as the bird matures. As this happens the bird starts breathing through its mouth and does so for the remainder of its life.

Anhingas have white markings on the back side of their wings and the male has an iridescent green sheen to its overall black color. Females have a light golden brown color on their neck and breast.

The Anhinga's long tail fans out to give it a nickname of "Water Turkey."

Swimming with its body submerged, only the Anhinga's long neck shows above the water, giving it another alias of "Snakebird".

Length: 34 to 36 inches.
Wingspan: 47 inches.
Habitat: Freshwater lakes, rivers, swamps and saltwater bays.
Season: Year round.
Field mark: Black shiny body with long straight bill.

Cormorant

The Double-crested Cormorant is similar to the Anhinga because it dives underwater for its food. They are able to fly when wet and, like the Anhinga, they prefer to dry their water-soaked feathers first. Airing their outstretched wings in the sun also acts as a solar collector for warmth after diving in cool water. Cormorants usually dive between 5 to 25 feet, but have been caught in fishing nets 100 feet below the surface and their underwater excursions last from 30 to 70 seconds. Large webbed feet make them good swimmers. They also use partially spread wings underwater to aid them in swimming, unlike Anhingas, which keep them close to their bodies. A hooked bill assures a tenacious grip on slippery fish: they prefer to surface before swallowing their catch. Like the Anhinga, when the Cormorant is young it breathes through its nostrils, but the bone structure soon grows together. Mature Cormorants and Anhingas then breathe through their mouths.

The Cormorant's turquoise eyes provide a jewel-like speck of color to its otherwise dark body.

A channel-mark perch is a favorite haunt of the Cormorant.

The unique Cormorant has been used by Asian fishermen for hundreds of years. A tight leash put around the bird's neck kept it from swallowing fish. As the bird surfaces, the owner would remove the fish from the Cormorant's throat, then the bird received every fifth fish or so as a reward. Today it is no longer economical, but Cormorants are still used in Japan as a curiosity to delight tourists.

The primitive-looking Cormorant is very heavy, and its wings are small in comparison to its weight. Momentary loss of altitude when taking off often causes its tail to dip into the water.

Length: 30 to 36 inches.
Wingspan: 50 inches.
Habitat: Ocean, salt- or freshwater bays, rivers and lakes.
Season: Year round.
Field mark: Hooked bill. Immature birds are brown; adults are black with yellowish orange throat pouch.

Coots, Gallinules and Common Moorhens

Coots, Gallinules and Common Moorhens look as though they would be closely related, and indeed they all belong to the family known as Rails. An interesting aspect of these birds is the shape of the head and bill, which are reminiscent of a cross between a duck and a chicken. Another feature is a unique forehead shield.

They feed on aquatic vegetation at freshwater marshes and lakes, where they characteristically bob their heads while swimming and walking on lily pads. These birds are not strong flyers. When taking off, they run across the water at a feverish pace until airborne. They are most frequently seen congregated together, although single birds will break off to find other ponds.

The Coot is a friendly waterbird with a white bill and a charcoal-colored body. Its large feet have unusual lobed "fingers."

Coot
Length: 13 to 16 inches.
Wingspan: 25 inches.
Habitat: Freshwater lakes, wetlands and saltwater bays.
Season: Year round, more common in winter.
Field mark: Blackish body with white bill.

The beautiful rich colors of the Purple Gallinule include almost every color on the artist's palette.

Purple Gallinule
Length: 11 to 13 inches.
Wingspan: 21 inches.
Habitat: Freshwater lakes and marshes.
Season: Year round.
Field mark: Purple coloring, red bill, bright yellow legs.

The Common Moorhen is most readily identified by its red forehead and bill with a yellow tip. Their overall dark body shows a flash of white on the flank.

Common Moorhen

Length: 11 to 13 inches.
Wingspan: 21 inches.
Habitat: Freshwater lakes and marshes.
Season: Year round.
Field mark: Bright red bill, dark brownish black body with white markings.

Clapper Rail

The Clapper Rail is a very secretive bird that rarely flies. More often heard than seen, they make a rasping "kek-kek-kek-kek" sound, like two stones being tapped together. Even though they are quite plentiful, you will be lucky to see one. Low sheltering branches of the mangroves along with tall marsh grass effectively hide them from sight. Their dark color also provides camouflage against the muddy floor of the areas where they dwell. Look for subtle movements in the marsh vegetation or a brief appearance while scurrying with a rapid jerky motion. In thick and dimly lit vegetation they sometimes can be mistaken for a rodent.

They eat crustaceans (crabs and shrimp), mollusks, (snails, oysters and clams) and an assortment of insects, frogs, aquatic plants, buds and seeds.

The best time to spot one is at high tide when they are darting between hiding places looking for food.

Length: 14 to 16 inches, about the size of a small chicken.

Wingspan: 20 inches.

Habitat: Dense vegetation of saltwater marshes.

Season: Year round.

Field mark: Tawny breast, long legs and curved bill.

Common Loon

Always alert, the loon can rear up for a look around.

The Common Loon visits Florida from November through March and sometimes stays into May. Traveling here in small flocks from their summer home in Canada and other northern areas, they migrate at night and are seldom seen flying.

It spends its life eating and sleeping on the open water. In its element, the Loon is a very skillful swimmer with strong webbed feet and thick oily plumage. Out of the water is a different story. The placement of their feet is so far back on their bodies, walking becomes almost impossible. Sliding on their bellies, they use their feet, wings and bills to propel them along.

Since flying is primarily at night, sometimes the black pavement of a parking lot looks much like water and the bird will land. They can only take off in water so when finding themselves in this peculiar situation they need the assistance of man to help them. Loons only come ashore to nest and always allow themselves easy access to the safety and security of the water.

The Loon has a daggerlike bill used when diving for small fish and crustaceans. If threatened, they will disappear underwater and swim away rather than take to the air.

Famous for its mournful cry, the Loon's voice carries for long distances over open water. Early sailors once believed that the call of the Loon foretold bad weather.

Length: 28 to 36 inches.
Wingspan: 58 inches.
Habitat: Open ocean and bays.
Season: Winter.
Field mark: Dark brownish gray above, white below. Straight bill.

Eagle

The portrait of the noble eagle is familiar in American folklore and is also a real part of Florida's environment.

The Bald Eagle is our national symbol, when seen in the wild provides a breathtaking memory. Along with the Osprey, the Eagle is a raptor, or bird of prey, feeding on larger fish taken from open freshwater lakes, rivers and saltwater bays. There is always a chance of spotting one of these magnificent birds, because Florida is home to more Eagles than any other state except Alaska.

With a life span of up to 50 years, Eagles mate for life. Some live here year round while others head north during the winter months, but they always return to the same nesting site. The nest is called an aerie and is made of sticks, usually in the top of a slash pine tree. Eagles repair and add to it each year. If they leave during the winter and their nest has been destroyed or taken over by Great Horned Owls, another nest is started. They can spend the entire breeding season building a new aerie instead of mating and raising young.

Immature Eagles are very dark in color for the first five years—lacking the white head and tail of an adult. Eagles have over 7,000 feathers which they spend several hours a day preening. This grooming is often done on a loafing perch overlooking a favorite expanse of fishing grounds.

Length: 30 to 43 inches.
Wingspan: 78 to 96 inches.
Habitat: Sea coasts, lakes and rivers.
Season: Year round, but more common in winter.
Field mark: Adult has white head and tail, very large brown body.

Great Egret

This stately white bird goes by various names. Sometimes called the American Egret, Common Egret, and White Egret, its official name is Great Egret. It is a common sight along Florida shores. Waterfront neighborhoods always have at least one of these friendly birds flying in daily for a handout of human food. They make their presence known and will even peck impatiently at a window to get attention. Most of the neighborhood Egrets are affectionately named by the people who feed them. When not getting someone's attention for a handout, they stalk their more natural diet of fish, crayfish, aquatic insects and frogs, which served them quite well long before there were hot dogs.

Befriending these alluring birds is unquestionably a source of enjoyment and satisfaction. It is difficult to resist feeding them, but in many ways does little to really help them and can sometimes be detrimental.

The Great Egret preens and flexes its wings to rearrange damaged feathers.

For example, an Egret comes to feed, the family dog chases it and the bird flies up and into a powerline breaking a wing. Wildlife rehabilitation centers receive many birds where just that sort of thing has happened. Through the use of good judgment and common sense both the birds and our own enthusiasm for them can be satisfied.

The Great Egret builds its nests in low mangroves, frequently within the colonies of other birds. The nest is approximately two feet wide and built of sticks and twigs. Three or four pale blue or green oval-shaped eggs are laid in the nest. Incubation lasts about 24 days and the young will fly 42 days after hatching.

In the late 19th century these birds, along with the Snowy Egret, were hunted almost to extinction for their plumage, which was used for hat decorations.

Length: 35 to 41 inches.
Wingspan: 55 inches.
Habitat: Marshes, banks or rivers, lakes and mangrove areas.
Season: Year round.
Field mark: All white body with yellow bill, black legs and feet.

The last thing an unwary fish might see is the uncanny stare of the Great Egret as it peers down from above.

Cattle Egret

During the mating season the Cattle Egret gets a buff-colored display of plumes on its crest, back and chest area.

Grazing livestock will stir up delicious insects as they walk along, making life easy for a hungry Cattle Egret.

This bird was originally from Southern Europe and Africa. They began to populate South America, moved north to the United States and were first seen here in 1952. Theories on how they got here vary from strong storms blowing them across the Atlantic to their being accidental stowaways aboard a freighter, but no one knows for sure.

You can see them almost anywhere in Florida. It could be along the side of the road, in a freshwater ditch or a saltwater bay, or of course in fields around livestock.

Diet consists of grasshoppers, frogs, snakes, small insects, and rodents. Extremely adaptable birds, these opportunists will follow a tractor or ride on the backs of cattle looking for food.

The Cattle Egret can sometimes be confused with the Snowy Egret. One difference lies in the color of their legs. The Cattle Egret has yellowish orange colored legs whereas the Snowy Egret has bright yellow feet with a yellow stripe up the back of its otherwise black legs. An exception to this is the immature Cattle Egret whose legs are darker. Another difference is that the bill of the Cattle Egret is yellow whereas the Snowy Egret's bill is primarily black. They build stick nests in low trees over the water and lay four light blue eggs.

Length: 20 inches.
Wingspan: 37 inches.
Habitat: Marshlands, prairies, and roadside ditches.
Season: Year round.
Field mark: White with yellow beak and legs.

Reddish Egret

The Reddish Egret lives primarily in the southern parts of Florida. Occasionally a few wander into the northern Gulf Coast areas. One of their strong features is the broad and shaggy plume feathers that adorn their head and neck.

Their feeding habits are quite unconventional. Most wading birds move slowly and deliberately when searching for small fish, and although the Reddish Egrets sometimes stand still, they more often than not hurtle recklessly about in shallow water with their wings spread. They frantically dance in no particular pattern in search of anything that moves. Their spread wings help prevent glare for a better look below the surface and may help in keeping their balance when leaping. All the time they are "rubber-legging" around looking as though they haven't a clue as to what they are doing, they are accurately stabbing fish and insects.

Not all Reddish Egrets are reddish. Some are entirely white, yet still are called Reddish Egrets. No one knows why these color "phases," as they are called, happen. Two reddish colored Egrets can mate and come up with a white bird, then a reddish and white can mate and have all white, all red or mixed and so on. The Reddish Egret is most prevalent and one thing they all have in common is a pinkish bill with a black tip.

They have never been quite as plentiful as the Great Egret and Snowy Egret but were a common sight until plume hunters killed most of them. One hopes that in the future their numbers will increase, but to date they have not made a very strong comeback.

Length: 25 to 30 inches.
Wingspan: 46 inches.
Habitat: Saltwater shallows and mangroves.
Season: Winter.
Field mark: Tawny red with shaggy crest and neck, pink-colored beak with black tip.

Snowy Egret

Unlike the Reddish Egret, the Snowy Egret is a little more organized in its feeding habits. It shuffles its feet quickly along the sandy bottom to drive small fish and crabs into the open, then stabs at them with its sharp beak. It is a frequent visitor to fishing piers and enjoys handouts almost as much as the Great Egret and the Brown Pelican. Identifying the Snowy Egret is easy. If it is wearing bright yellow "snow shoes," then it's a Snowy Egret. A thin yellow stripe also runs up the back side of otherwise black legs. Their bills are black, unlike the Cattle Egret, whose bill is a yellowish orange color.

The mating plumage of the Snowy Egret is magnificent. There is no way to adequately depict the elegance and beauty of their delicate feathers.

At the turn of the century, hunters supplied milliners with plume feathers that were much in demand for decorating hats. This went on until these attractive birds were almost extinct. In 1886 the Audubon Society was founded and started the protection of non-game birds especially over the plumage issue. Today it is illegal to wear or even possess a single wild bird feather no matter how common or insignificant the feather may appear.

The Snowy Egret likes to nest in shrubs and low trees and its colonies can sometimes contain several thousand birds. Eggs will incubate in 18 days and the hatchlings will fly in three weeks.

Length: 20 to 27 inches.
Wingspan: 38 inches.
Habitat: Marshlands, mangroves, freshwater lakes and rivers.
Season: Year round.
Field mark: Snowy white feathers, black bill, black legs with yellow feet.

Flamingo

The Flamingo has been a symbol of Florida since early tourist days, yet it is not even remotely part of the Florida bird community today. At the turn of the century flocks of Flamingos were in Florida and Louisiana, but haven't been here since that time. If you see one in the wild it has most likely escaped from a tourist attraction.

The State of Florida uses the Flamingo in its advertising as if it were the only bird here. With all the gorgeous birds that grace the water's edge in this state, it is hard to understand why they use a bird that is native to the islands of the Caribbean to promote Florida.

The most famous of Flamingo stories took place at the horse racing track at Hialeah Park near Miami. Some people thought it would be a good idea to grace the inner circle of the track with a flock of these intriguing birds. They soon brought back Flamingos from Cuba, but because their wings were not clipped or pinioned, the Flamingos flew away the very next day. Sightings of the birds in that area were frequent for some time but they were never seen back at the park. In 1937 they tried again, this time fixing the wing problem. Flamingos have been there ever since and each year an average of 80 young are raised, bringing their total to over 800.

In captivity, the Flamingo needs a special diet of carotene to maintain their bright pink color, otherwise they will turn light pink to white. In the wild they feed on organic matter and small animals while wading, providing themselves with needed nutrients.

The Flamingo lowers its head and swishes through the mud, feeding with its bill upside down. The tongue acts like a piston, bringing water in and out of the bill 3 or 4 times a second, straining out organisms with comb-like filters just inside the bill. It has the longest neck of any bird in the world compared to its body size and it is the only wading bird with webbed feet.

Care and preening of feathers are a constant job for all birds. The Flamingo's flexible neck can look like a garden hose out of control when performing this chore.

Length: 48 inches.
Wingspan: 55 inches.
Habitat: Caribbean areas.
Not normally found in the wild in Florida.

Frigatebird

The Magnificent Frigatebird has a reputation for boldly harassing other birds that are carrying fish while in flight. This intimidation goes on to the point where the upset bird simply drops its catch and flies on. The Frigatebird then swoops down to retrieve the fish in midair, earning not only a free meal but its nickname, Man-o'-war. All the same, they are quite able to seize fish, squid, jellyfish and young sea turtles from the water. Frigatebirds also feed on other colonies of nesting birds, including their own. In cannibalistic fashion they circle overhead watching for young chicks that have been left unattended.

Gracefully soaring Frigatebirds look almost like fanciful oriental kites as they float in the air.

Most people think Frigatebirds stay out over the ocean, but in fact they seldom leave the sight of land. They are, however, one of the world's most impressive flyers, and can effortlessly soar for hours at a time on wind currents. They will not land in the water as their feathers quickly get waterlogged, making flight impossible. They are equally inept and clumsy on land. Without a strong wind, they have trouble getting airborne from a beach. Consequently they roost in trees or rocks where they can gain better air speed at take off.

Distinctive features include a scissorlike forked tail and long angled wings. The male has a brilliant red throat pouch which is inflated to enormous proportions during courtship. The females have a white chest and the immature birds have an all-white head. Ordinarily Frigatebirds are seen in Florida during the summer months, though some stay all winter.

The reproductive rate of the Frigatebird is low and breeding doesn't start until about age seven. Only one egg is laid and, 100 days after it has hatched, the male will abandon the nest, leaving the female to raise the young.

Worldwide there are five species of Frigatebirds, but only the Magnificent Frigatebird is native to Florida.

Length: 38 to 41 inches.

Wingspan: 7 to 8 feet, yet weighs only 3 go 4 pounds. This makes their plane-surface-to-weight ratio greater than any other bird.

Habitat: Along seacoasts.

Season: Summer and fall.

Field mark: Deeply forked tail and long angled wings.

Gulls

The most common bird by the shore is the Gull. If you want to see one, just spread a picnic basket out on the beach and in an instant they will appear in droves even when none were anywhere in sight just a moment before.

Technically there is no such bird as a "seagull," and many dictionaries don't include the word. They are simply Gulls. They are found in every country of the world and all told there are 43 species.

Gulls enjoy shellfish and will drop them from heights onto parking lots to break the shell. They quickly follow it down to prevent a fellow Gull from getting it first. In addition to wanting whatever you are eating, they are satisfied with practically anything and in garbage sites they are king of the heap.

Not good fishermen but great scavengers, Gulls help keep our beaches clean of dead fish and garbage.

Herring Gull

The Herring Gull visits during the cooler months and it derives its name from its large appetite for herring. It is one of the larger Gulls and has an unmistakable and characteristic shriek that can carry a great distance.
It mates for life and returns to the same nesting site every year. Nests are often on the ground, built up of sticks and grasses then lined with soft feathers.

Length: 22 to 26 inches.
Wingspan: 54 inches.
Habitat: Coastal seashores and inland.
Season: Winter.
Field mark: White with gray back, wing tips are black with white spots.

Laughing Gull

The Laughing Gull is the most common Gull seen in Florida and lives here year round. Since their plumage changes dramatically from summer to winter, many people think they are two different Gulls. In the winter months, their heads are white whereas in the summer, which is their mating season, they have a hood of jet black with little white "eyeglasses." One feature Gulls have in common is that they all have white on them no matter what variety. The only exceptions are immature gulls, which are brown.

Although they are able fishermen, Gulls would rather scavenge for food. They will even alight on the head of a pelican to grab a fish from its mouth. The Laughing Gull's domain extends inland, benefitting farmers by eating beetles, grasshoppers, cockroaches, moths and many crop-destroying insects. Its name comes from the crazed sounding laugh heard so often along beaches and harbors.

Length: 15 to 17 inches.
Wingspan: 41 inches.
Habitat: Coastal beaches, shorelines and bays. Less common inland.
Season: Year round.
Field mark: Black head in summer, white with gray in winter.

Ring-billed Gull

Gulls can easily catch bits of food tossed into the air.

The Ring-billed Gull is a winter visitor arriving in Florida during October. Some linger here all year round, but most head north in early May. They are masters of the wind currents and can soar without flapping a wing. Inland, they follow the farmer's plow, picking up insects, and will even feed on small game such as mice. About half their food is comprised of fish, the other half is refuse and insects. They can be found in most parts of the country.

Length: 18 to 21 inches.
Wingspan: 49 inches.
Habitat: Seacoasts and inland.
Season: Winter.
Field mark: Black band on bill.

Great Blue Heron

Once in flight, the Great Blue Heron's neck is folded into an "S". All Herons share this trait. Once underway they can reach speeds of 30 m.p.h.

The Great Blue Heron is a solitary and stoic hunter of the shallows. It feeds in the daytime and at night, standing motionlessly in the water until a fish swims within striking distance. As quick as any rattlesnake, the Heron's head will thrust forward to nab its unwary prey. It will then flip the fish into the air, catch it head first and swallow it whole.

The Heron will often subdue a large and unwieldy fish by slapping it against the water or shore. These capable stalkers also like frogs, snakes and even small birds. Strange as it may seem, if a Heron has a choice between eating a fish or a mouse, it will choose the mouse first.

Their voice is very raucous and guttural and they normally call out when taking to the air. Wing beats are very even and deliberate when flying, making the total countenance of this wonderful bird impressive and majestic.

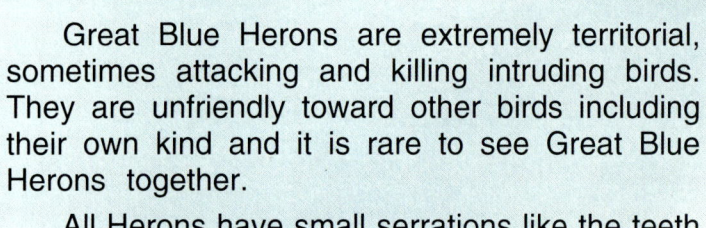

Great Blue Herons are extremely territorial, sometimes attacking and killing intruding birds. They are unfriendly toward other birds including their own kind and it is rare to see Great Blue Herons together.

All Herons have small serrations like the teeth of a comb on the side of their middle claw. It is used to aid in preening in places where the Heron cannot reach with its bill. Special feathers which crumble into powder are rubbed onto the claw and the powder aids in cleaning.

Birds encounter many hazards by man, predators and other forces of nature. In 1935, the Labor Day hurricane devastated the Great Blue Heron colonies. In the Florida Keys only sixty of these princely birds survived.

The Great Blue Heron is very aristocratic and dominates the edges of lakes and marshes with its bossy and noisy disposition.

Length: 39 inches.
Wingspan: Can reach almost 7 feet.
Habitat: All wetlands.
Season: Year round.
Field mark: White head with bold black stripe, body is overall grayish.

Tricolored Heron

Once called the Louisiana Heron, the Tricolored Heron fishes the bays and inlets looking for fish, frogs, and any other aquatic life found in the areas it haunts. They also like small animals, mice and insects.

From the back it can sometimes be mistaken for the Little Blue Heron. If you look to the front of its neck for identification you will see a herringbone pattern of white feathers down the entire length. They also have a white underside.

The Tricolored Heron is a patient and precise stalker of small fish.

"Lady of the waters" was a term of endearment used by Audubon for this graceful bird and is still used today by naturalists.

The Tricolored Heron builds a nest of sticks and lays three to four beautiful powder-blue eggs, which take about 21 days to hatch. I have been in tourist areas where these birds were nesting a few feet away from where hundreds of people walk by and it doesn't seem to bother them. When need be, they share a similar trait with the Bittern by facing their enemy with beak straight up and neck extended, blending in with the surrounding reeds.

Length: 25 to 30 inches.
Wingspan: 38 inches.
Habitat: Mangroves, salt- and fresh-water shorelines.
Season: Year round.
Field mark: Blue gray coloring with white herringbone pattern under neck and white underparts.

Little Blue Heron

The Little Blue Heron is a distinct species of the Heron family and not just a small version of the Great Blue Heron. This amusing little Heron is a common prowler of shorelines in our state. Not having the exotic mating plumage of the other Herons and Egrets, their population was never affected by the plume hunters at the turn of the century. Its range extends along the Atlantic seaboard and up the Mississippi, but it is most abundant in Florida and around the Gulf of Mexico.

Favorite foods include small fish and aquatic animals, but insects make up a larger part of their diet. When a lucrative feeding area is discovered, a Little Blue Heron will return daily to feed and stand guard as long as the food supply is plentiful.

Being a shy bird, the Little Blue Heron can be difficult to get close to, but from a distance it can be observed working its way along a shoreline searching and poking in every hiding place that might harbor a frog or dragonfly. Nests are made of sticks and nesting sites are chosen in bushes or small trees.

The Little Blue Heron has a dark slate-colored body and maroonish brown neck. Its bill is gray with a black tip and the legs are a greenish color. The immature Little Blue Heron is solid white for two years. Until then it can easily be confused with the Snowy Egret. If the legs are a greenish color, then it is probably an immature Little Blue. Remember, the Snowy Egret is wearing yellow "snow shoes" and has a solid black beak.

Color changes occur in many birds between their immature and adult years, but none so dramatic as with the Little Blue Heron.

Length: 25 to 30 inches.
Wingspan: 41 inches.
Habitat: Fresh- and saltwater marshes, mangroves and lakes.
Season: Year round.
Field mark: Adult, all slate blue. Immature, white, gray legs and bill.

45

Great White Heron

There are a lot of questions about the Great White Heron that have yet to be answered. They have been found in the nests of Great Blue Herons, which would lead you to think they are a color accident of nature. In scientific terms this is called a "phase" or "morph." Yet the Great White Heron cannot be found anywhere except southern Florida and a few places in the Caribbean. Since the range of the Great Blue Heron covers most of the United States, why then is the Great White only found within such a specific area? No one knows, and it remains a mystery, as do so many of the habits and lives of so many birds.

The Great White Heron National Refuge in the Keys is a haven that has been set aside for this stately species rarely seen in most parts of Florida.

The Great White Heron's difference in attitude further set them apart from the Great Blue Heron. Neither are friendly birds even to their own kind, but the Great White Heron is more disagreeable. Their disposition is ruthless towards others and they will even strike at full-grown fowls and ducks, which they can tear apart and eat.

The Great White Heron tends to be somewhat larger than the Great Blue Heron and of course as with any species of bird, some may occasionally wander far away from their usual haunts. Their already small population has sometimes been further reduced by powerful hurricanes. Unless you're close to them, they can easily be mistaken for Great Egrets, but they have yellow legs whereas the Egret has black legs.

Length: 50 inches.
Wingspan: 70 inches.
Habitat: Mangroves and coastal shorelines.
Season: Year round.
Field mark: All white with yellow beak and legs.

Yellow-crowned Night Heron

The quiet Yellow-crowned Night Heron can most often be seen passively resting along the shoreline rather than actively feeding. More likely the Yellow-crowned Night Heron is actually waiting for sundown, because these are the birds that work the second shift, feeding at twilight and at night. In this way they avoid territorial disputes with other birds that might occur during the day. They are not, however, strictly limited to nocturnal feeding, and sometimes can be seen during the day searching for crabs and small fish. Crabs make up such a large part of their diet that they have been nicknamed the "crab eater."

Small fish make a good variation from the more common diet of shallow-water crabs.

This distinguished-looking bird does not readily mix with other herons, preferring its own company. The Yellow-crowned Night Heron nest in small villages of their own species, including immature birds of a year or so old. The paired adults choose nesting sites in April or early May that are at the water's edge but high enough in the trees to be out of the reach of alligators and other predators. Both parents share incubation, and when the chicks are hatched, the adults provide shade by spreading a fan of special breeding plumes.

Length: 22 to 27 inches.
Wingspan: 44 inches.
Habitat: Marshlands and mangroves.
Season: Year round.
Field mark: Black-and-white striped face.

Black-crowned Night Heron

This handsome bird is not as frequently seen as the Yellow-crowned Night Heron. It is stalkier and in many ways takes on a more stately appearance with its solid colors. As its name implies, it too hunts for food in the evening or at dusk, but otherwise is quite inactive. When feeding at the edge of a mangrove shore or swampy area it will stand perfectly still with its head drawn down between its shoulders. As an unsuspecting fish or frog wanders by, the Heron strikes with lightning speed. Other food includes snakes, insects, crustaceans, small birds, mammals and occasionally the nestling of a neighboring Heron.

It raises its family in large colonies, often among other nesting birds like the Great Blue Heron and Green-backed Heron. This proximity to others during mating season brings on a constant ruckus of noise and feuding. They feed both day and night during this time until the voracious young can fly.

The plumage of the immature Night Heron is markedly different during the first year.

Length: 23 to 28 inches.
Wingspan: 44 inches.
Habitat: Fresh- and saltwater marshes.
Season: Year round.
Field mark: Glossy black crown with short neck, gray wings and white underparts.

Green-backed Heron

A very small Heron, it has an unusual ability to stretch its neck to quite remarkable lengths from what appears to be no neck at all when retracted. That comes in quite handy while catching fish. All Herons are good fishermen, waiting patiently for fish to swim by, but the Green-backed Heron uses its "head" as well as its bill when catching fish. It sometimes catches a small insect and uses it as bait by placing it in the water. If the insect starts to drift away the Heron will pick it up and place it back in position. When a fish comes close enough to get interested in the insect, it ends up as a meal for the Heron. They have also been seen taking scraps of bread and using them the same way. If no fish comes around they will take up their loaf and move it to a more promising spot—as any good fisherman would. These same birds have been photographed using a small down feather in their bills as a lure. It is very unusual for any animal to use tools like this, and in some respects it shows the intelligence of this bird. In other ways the Green-backed Heron seems a little dim-witted. After eating it will often go to sleep and remain motionless until a person or predator almost steps on it.

When feeding, the Green-backed Heron has a cat-like approach. It takes slow cautious steps and before striking twitches its tail.

The Green-backed Heron is a solitary bird that as a rule stays out of population's way. When alarmed, it will twitch its tail feathers nervously, then sound out with a boisterous squawk as it flies off. Upon landing, it will still be twitching its tail with its neck still outstretched. Its eyes will be moving in all directions searching for the source of whatever startled it.

These Herons nest from March to June in single pairs, generally not in colonies. Herons are not known as great nest builders and the Green-backed Heron's nest is probably the worst. It is flat with no rim and so poorly built that eggs and young birds easily fall out. Three or four delicate greenish blue eggs are laid.

Length: 16 to 22 inches.
Wingspan: 25 inches.
Habitat: Banks of lakes, rivers and saltwater shorelines.
Season: Year round.
Field mark: Dark green back, chestnut-colored neck and orange-yellow legs.

Würdemann's Heron

Southernmost Florida and the Keys are home to the Würdemann's Heron. This large and rare Florida Heron is a color variation of the Great Blue Heron. As with other Herons, the Würdemann's hunts for prey in knee-deep water. It is always alert and watchful of its surroundings and the least sign of danger will cause it to take flight. Tall cypress trees in the Everglades are preferred for nesting, as well as black mangrove trees off Cape Sable.

Early settlers in South Florida cited the Würdemann's Heron as a raider of chicken farms, picking up young chicks and swallowing them as fast as it could. Persecution for this reason may be why we don't have an abundant population of this majestic Heron today.

Stately and keen-eyed, the Würdemann's Heron is very similar to the Great Blue Heron but lacks the bold black marking on its head.

Length: 50 to 52 inches.
Wingspan: 77 to 82 inches.
Habitat: Mangroves and shorelines in Florida Keys.
Season: Year round.
Field mark: Gray coloring with white head and throat.

American Bittern

This solitary bird lives a hermitlike existence in marshes and in the reeds of lakes and quiet rivers. Spending most of its life on the ground, the American Bittern seldom lights on trees or even small bushes. It is so elusive you will rarely see one, even though it could be living only a few feet away. A master of camouflage, it has coloring to match the yellows and browns of the surrounding reeds and grasses. Instead of flying to safety, the Bittern will point its bill and neck straight up and freeze in the reeds, making it almost impossible to see. Its unusual strategy doesn't stop there. Standing perfectly still could be a danger in itself if the reeds around the Bittern were moving in the breeze. Instinctively knowing this, the Bittern will mimic swaying reeds by moving from side to side right along with the foliage. However, if danger comes too close, it will abruptly take to the air with a loud croak to surprise the intruder.

Even with their nest sites they are very cautious. Several trails go out from the nest among the reeds and they never fly directly to or from it. Instead, the parents will land up to thirty feet away, then slowly and cautiously follow one of their trails in. This maneuver helps to bewilder any would-be intruder like a hawk from finding the nest. When leaving they will always use a different trail out from the one they came in on and take wing only after they are some distance away.

They have a strange call that can travel long distances over the calm marshlands. Its eerie sound is like that of someone laboring with a hammer or mallet, giving them nicknames such as "Thunder-pumper" and "Stake-driver." This call has probably been responsible for more than one swamp legend. Its diet includes small aquatic animals with frogs and grasshoppers a favorite.

Cloaked with the patterns and colors of the reeds, the Bittern strikes a pose to blend in with the landscape.

Length: 23 to 24 inches.
Wingspan: 45 inches.
Habitat: Thick marsh grasses and reeds.
Season: Mostly winter but some year round.
Field mark: Brown streaks and general stocky appearance.

White Ibis

A very social bird among its own kind, the White Ibis can be instantly recognized by its long downward-curved red bill and bright red legs. They nest in large colonies and feed together on muddy or sandy shores. The Ibis uses its curved bill to probe around vegetation and into the soft mud. Feeding more by touch than by sight, they specialize in crayfish and fiddler crabs.

Ibis also like small fish, snails, insects, grasshoppers and snakes. During early morning and at sunset you may see them flying in formation. Small groups travel between the feeding grounds and their inland roost up to 15 miles away.

Length: 23 to 27 inches.
Wingspan: 38 inches.
Habitat: Coastal and freshwater shorelines, mud flats and mangroves.
Season: Year round.
Field mark: All white, red legs and red face with long down-curved bill.

The immature Ibis loses its drab colors as it comes into adult plumage.

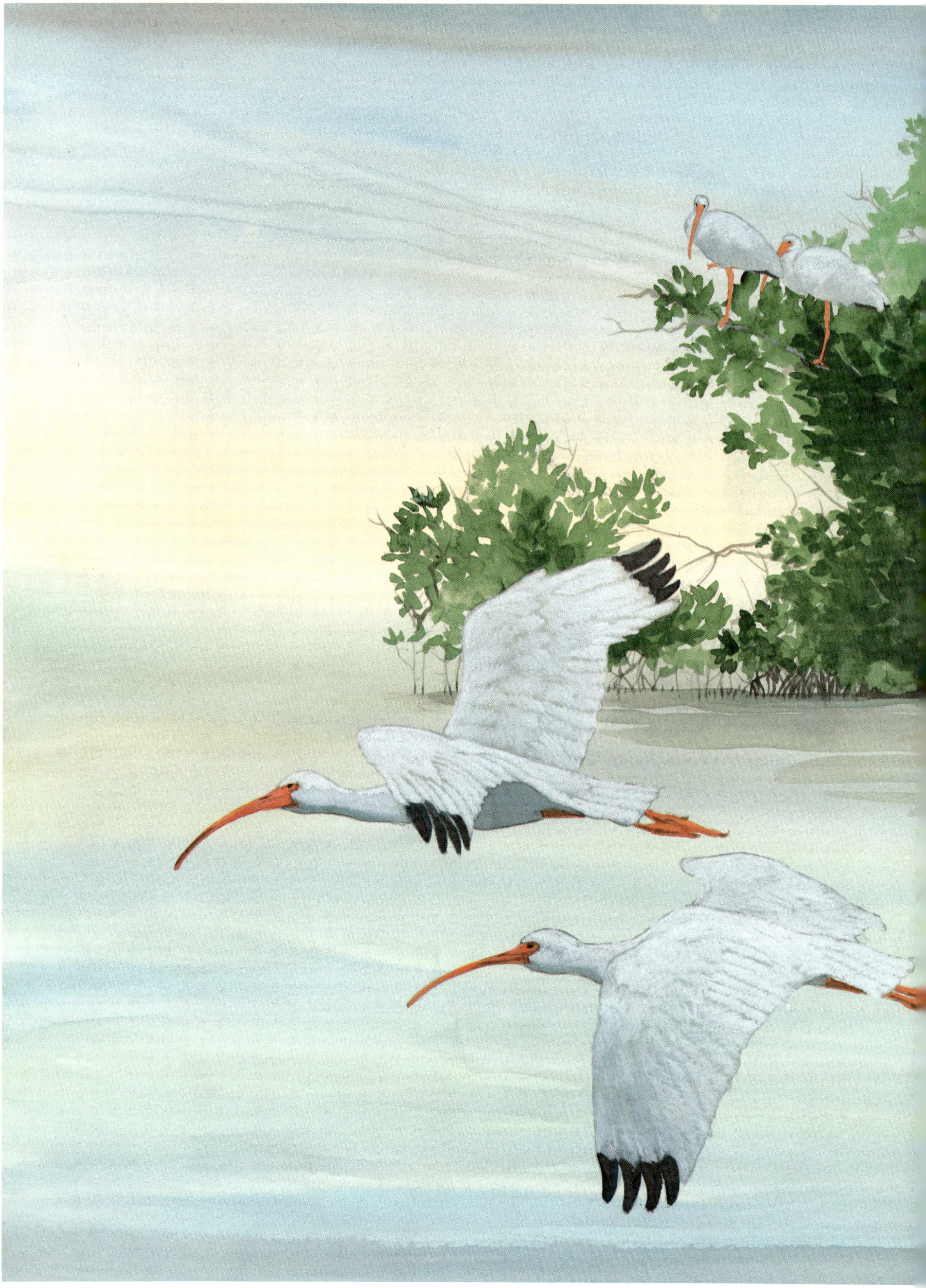

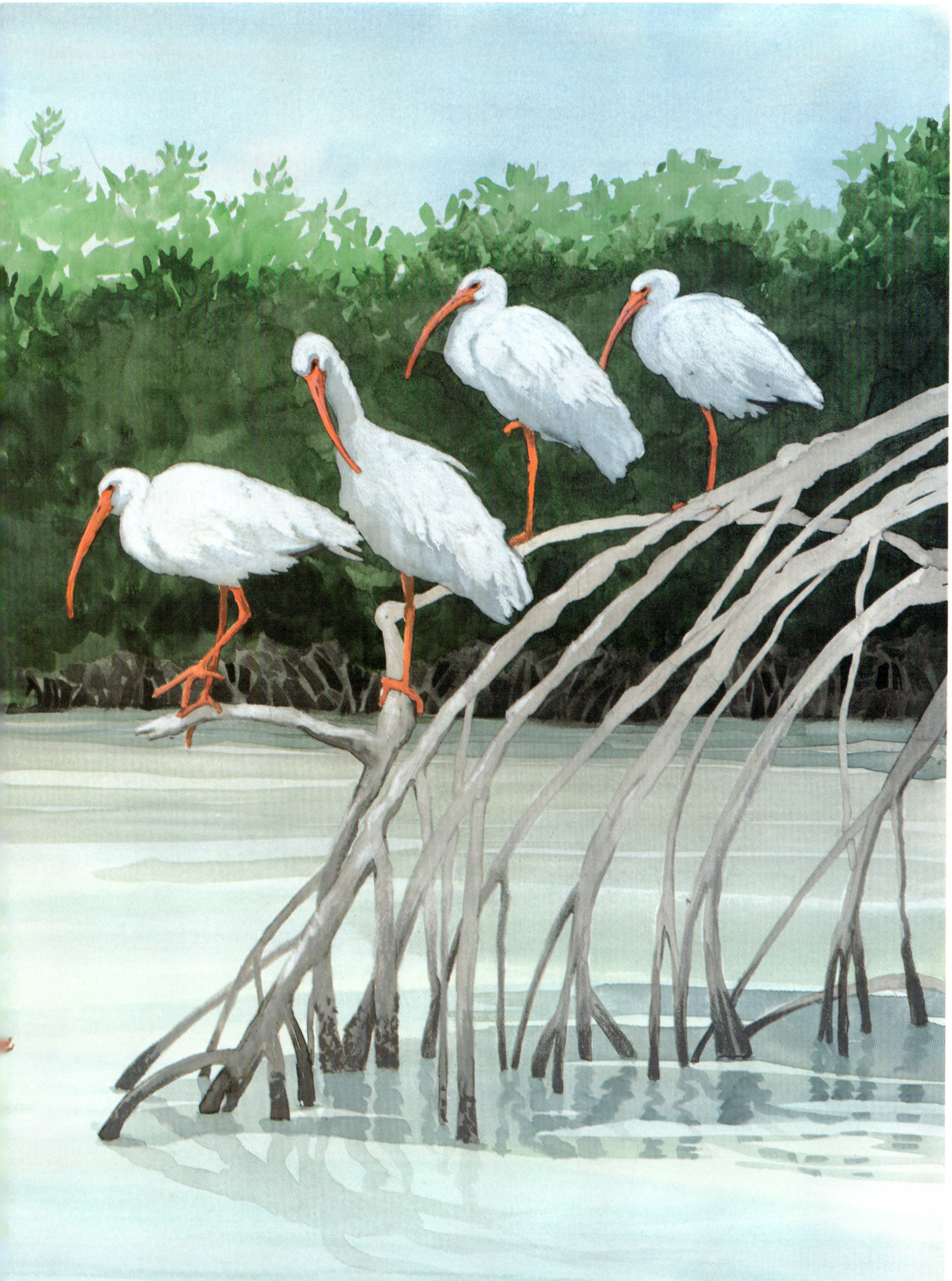

Glossy Ibis

John James Audubon wrote from St. Augustine in 1832, "Glossy Ibis is of exceedingly rare occurrence in the United States where it appears only at long and irregular intervals like a wanderer who has lost his way."

The Glossy Ibis, with its chestnut-bronze and translucent green feathers on its wings, is a lovely sight—if you are lucky enough to see one. It's not that they are as rare as they once were when Audubon was alive, but they do shy away from areas that are populated. From a distance they can be mistaken for the Curlew as they appear quite dark, almost black in color.

They feed mainly on fiddler crabs but also eat fish, insects, and snakes, including poisonous ones like the water moccasin.

The Glossy Ibis just arrived from Africa during the last century, which is partly the reason their population is small.

Length: 22 to 25 inches.
Wingspan: 37 inches.
Habitat: Marshlands.
Season: Year round.
Field mark: Dark green and violet feathers and curved bill.

Habitats
Mangroves

Mangrove areas are among the most important habitats in Florida and are primarily found in the southern half of the state. They stabilize the shoreline by preventing erosion and become a nursery for all kinds of fish, shellfish and crustaceans. When mangroves are disturbed or destroyed, the chain of life is affected. From the small larvae of marine life such as shrimp, the impact continues up the ladder to the nesting sites of large birds, such as Pelicans and Egrets.

Commercial and sport fishing are directly affected by the tampering of mangrove areas, as this is where the spawning of the first food chains begin. Where there are few fish, there will be few birds, and on it goes.

There are three types of mangroves. The red mangrove, sometimes called the walking tree, lives in the water and gives young fish and sea creatures an excellent place to hide and breed. Their branches are ideal for cradling the nests of many of Florida's birds. During the summer, pencil shaped pods called propagules develop on the branches. They drop off and stick in the mud to root or float away to propagate somewhere else.

The black mangrove grows back from the water's edge just a bit. It has hundreds of fingerlike projections coming up from around its root system which supply oxygen to the plant. Mangroves have the unusual ability to deal with the problems of salt water. In the black mangrove, salt is secreted through the leaves, making the underside coated with powdery salt.

The red mangrove blocks salt absorption at its roots. Another type of mangrove, the white mangrove, lives still further back from the shore and provides more excellent nesting habitats.

Florida regulates the cutting and removal of mangroves. Heavy fines of up to $10,000 per day per offense can be levied for violations. This gives you an idea of the importance of this wonderful resource.

Ocean Beaches

Where the open sea meets the land there runs a ribbon of sandy beaches and mud flats that supports large populations of shorebirds, Skimmers, Gulls and Terns.

In the surf, breakers are constantly depositing organisms on the sand, providing a wealth of food for Sandpipers and other shorebirds. On the mud flats, the ebb and flow of the tide renews the feeding grounds for Ibis, Spoonbills, and Storks.

Though vulnerable to the weather, many seabirds and shorebirds nest on the sand or in the grass above the high-water line.

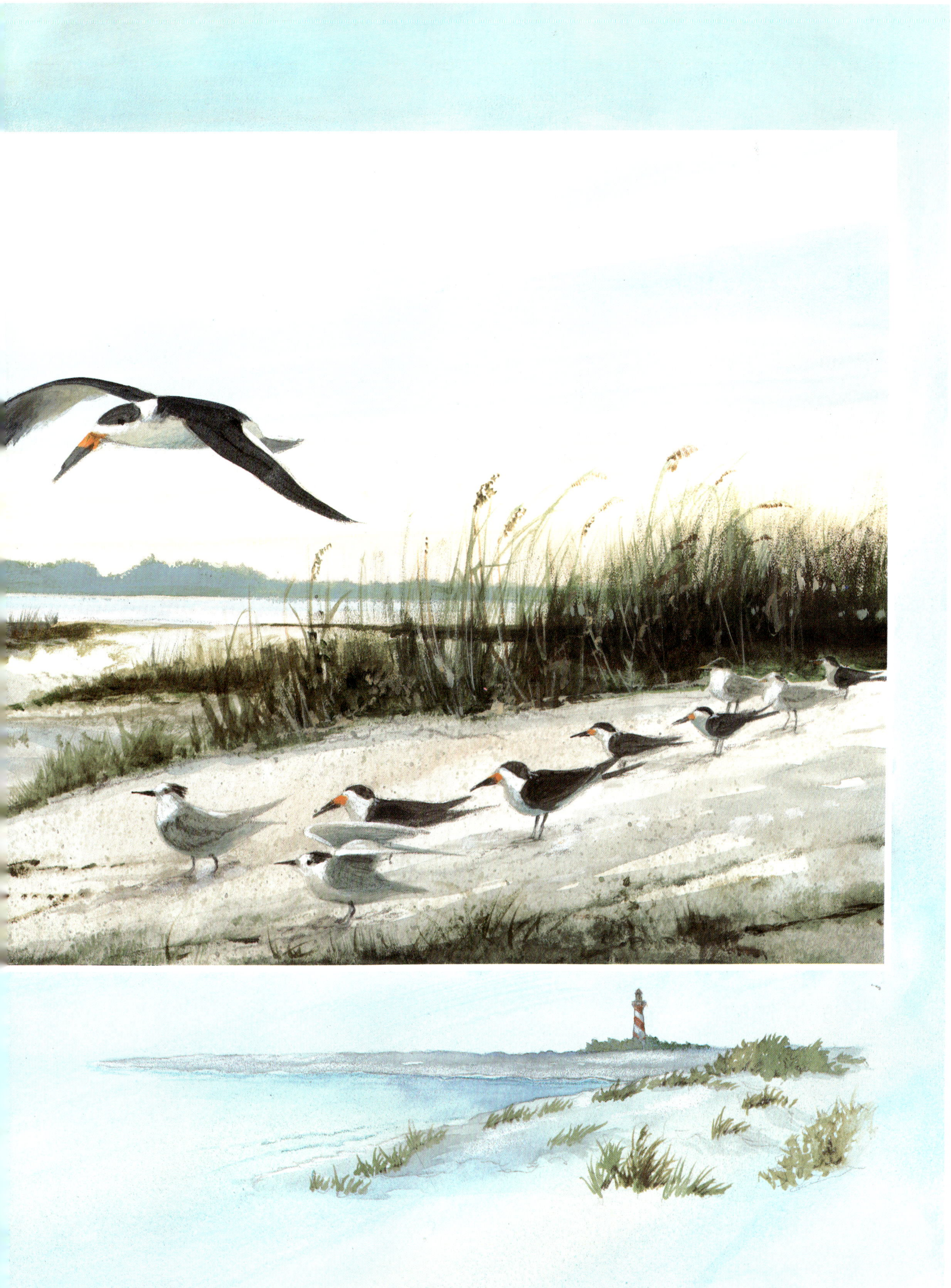

Marshlands

The salt marsh is another important coastal community producing large amounts of organic nutrients essential to the nourishment of bays. These areas go largely unnoticed by most people because they look uninviting with their soft, black, muddy bottoms.

For a salt marsh to occur, the land must be flat and the tidal action quiet. As sediments collect, specialized grasses take hold and trap even more sediments to create muddy bottom environments. These areas cannot tolerate strong tidal action but need the slight scouring effect from quiet tides.

The plant-oriented salt marshes take up where mangrove coastlines end and are essential in providing nutrients to marine plants and shellfish, as well as some invertebrates and fin fish. Many birds, including Willets, Storks, Night Herons and the elusive Clapper Rail, all inhabit this indispensable resource.

Open Ocean

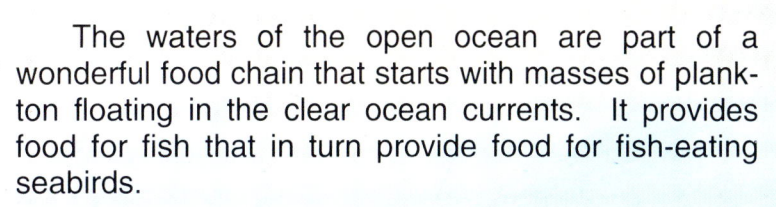

The waters of the open ocean are part of a wonderful food chain that starts with masses of plankton floating in the clear ocean currents. It provides food for fish that in turn provide food for fish-eating seabirds.

Open ocean birds such as the Loon choose to live at sea, only coming ashore for nesting, on islands and undisturbed shorelines. Other birds like the Sandwich Tern, Sooty Tern, Brown Pelican, and Gull fly over this demanding environment.

Birds often land on passing ships, driftwood or even clumps of seaweed to rest. Many miles away from shore, seabirds have learned to follow fishing boats, scavenging for scraps thrown overboard. On the other hand, the captains of fishing boats have known for centuries to look for congregations of feeding birds to locate schools of fish.

Estuaries

An estuary is where rivers and bays meet. The mixture of salt water at high tide and brackish water at low tide produces marshlands and rich feeding grounds for many animals. Deposits of silt by rivers give rich nutrients for plant growth and the muddy bottom supplies a banquet of small crustaceans and insects.

Here are the nursery environments for juvenile shell and fin fish as well as food resources for those young fish. The relative shallowness of an estuary provides good feeding opportunities for shorebirds, Herons and Egrets.

Mangroves and islands offer birds undisturbed areas where there are few predators. Spoil islands made from the excess sand of dredged channels have become excellent places for nesting birds. Man however, appears the worst enemy of our Florida birds. Years ago hunting almost wiped out many species; today population growth and development have taken its place. Interference, though not malicious, has caused some bird colonies to diminish or disappear. Awareness by concerned citizens and tourists can play a major part in keeping Florida healthy.

Florida is fortunate to have an abundance of bays—especially on the west coast. Estuaries offer food, shelter and nesting areas for birds and with our help they will remain that way.

Cypress Swamps

Stands of cypress trees are captivating scenes of beauty that flourish in the humid climate of Florida. Many birds utilize cypress tree canopies for nesting. Rookeries of the Wood Stork and the Great Blue Heron are common. Cypress swamps or "domes" may not always be large and are often scattered within larger freshwater habitats. The quiet dark waters provide rich feeding areas for species such as the elusive Limpkin as it searches for snails.

Lakes and Rivers

These bodies of open water offer feeding areas for birds that swim or dive for fish and a safe haven of quiet shorelines where birds can rest and preen. It is a good opportunity to observe Florida birds firsthand. Many Great Egrets have become so accustomed to people around lakes that hand feeding them is often possible. It can be a memorable experience for small children growing up, inspiring an interest and concern that might remain throughout their life.

Shorelines provide good hunting for Herons and excellent nesting for Ospreys and Cormorants.

Prairies

There are, technically speaking, two types of prairies—the wet prairie and the dry prairie. The wet prairie is dominated by grassy vegetation and is usually distinguished from marshes by having less water and shorter grass. Their dominant features are sawgrass, cordgrass and rushes. This provides abundant feeding and undisturbed habitat for Sandhill Cranes, Storks, Herons, Ibis and Egrets. The Everglades are wet prairies in the interior of the state with mangrove swamp along the coast. The Everglades are often referred to as "A river of grass." The Seminoles called it "Pa-Hay-Okee," which means grassy waters. This river is a slow movement of fresh water southward toward the Gulf of Mexico. The grassy prairie is dotted with low islands of willows, bay trees, cypress domes and palmetto hammocks.

Dry prairies are areas with sandy soil where saw palmettos are the dominant vegetation and is a preferred habitat for the Sandhill Crane. During the dry winter season the brown grasses will often be swept by wild fire. This cycle enables rich nutrients to break down and renews the prairie with abundant growth in the spring.

Kingfisher

The Kingfisher qualifies as the most timid bird in our book. Getting close to one is just about impossible. Their shrill and distinctive cry, which sounds like the harsh rattle from a New Year's noisemaker, can alert you to their presence as they rocket along a creek. They are extremely fast and strong flyers and the instant you appear, they disappear, flying off in the other direction.

These portly little birds like to sit motionless on telephone wires or fence posts near the water, watching for prey. When the Kingfisher spots something edible, it will dive and grab with its strong beak, then fly back to the perch with its food. Their flight is a succession of very rapid wing strokes and then short glides with a noticeable drop in altitude with wings partially closed. Hovering above the water with its bill pointed downward is another way the Kingfisher feeds, waiting for a fish to come to the surface. They also eat crustaceans, reptiles, amphibians and many insects.

Being cavity dwellers by nature, Kingfishers live by creek banks burrowing tunnels into the dirt and sand. Their large bill is used to start the operation, but most of the work is done with disproportionately tiny feet comprised of partially joined toes, two pointing forward and two back. Their feet are so small, it is hard to understand how any digging can be accomplished at all, yet their tunnels can extend from three to ten feet in length and always end in a round chamber. The Kingfisher will typically plunge into the creek upon emerging from its tunnel to clean its feathers from the leftover scraps of fish, dirt and the mess their young leave behind.

The female has two bands of color across her chest, one rusty and the other a blue-gray. The male's chest has a single blue-gray band.

The steep embankment of a stream provides privacy and concealment for the Kingfisher's tunnel.

Length: 11 to 13 inches.
Habitat: Lake and river banks and sometimes saltwater shorelines.
Season: Year round.
Field mark: Large bill and head for body size, fuzzy crest.

Limpkin

If you are walking near a freshwater lake or marsh and find apple snail shells and opened freshwater clams on the edge of the bank, chances are Limpkins live close by. They never stray far from this primary diet. The snail is carried to shore where the Limpkin holds it upside down using its long toes. With nimble dexterity it removes the snail's trap door and quickly pulls the mollusk out of its shell to be eaten.

Frogs, tadpoles and small aquatic insects are also a part of their diet. They live principally in Florida, with a few in Georgia, but always around fresh water. These birds do not migrate and have not developed good flying skills. The name Limpkin comes from their faltering walk that makes them appear injured.

The Limpkin is chiefly nocturnal and has a harsh, eerie, almost human wail that gives the Limpkin its nickname "crying bird." It will call out especially at night and can keep up its startling vocal display for long periods of time.

Apple snails make up the largest part of the Limpkins' diet to the extent that they cannot survive without them. If a marsh is drained and the snails disappear, so will the Limpkins.

Length: 25 to 28 inches.
Wingspan: 42 inches.
Habitat: Wooded swamps.
Season: Year round.
Field mark: Down-curved bill, brown with white markings.

Osprey

One of the most spectacular birds, the Osprey lives near the open water. Although there are many Ospreys in our state, they are not exclusive to Florida. They inhabit every continent in the world except the Antarctic.

Singly or in pairs, Ospreys will typically soar and circle high over a lake or bay searching with their keen eyesight. When a meal-sized fish shows itself on the surface, the Osprey folds in its wings and starts a daredevil dive. Instead of using its hawklike beak to grasp a fish, the Osprey will sink its razor-sharp talons with spiny grippers into its prey at the moment of contact, insuring a firm hold. The splash and struggle of an Osprey flying off with a mullet or a large-mouth bass in its talons is one of nature's best free shows.

The Osprey flies to the nest or a nearby dead tree to eat. There it works the fish into smaller pieces to be shared with its young—not yet able to swallow fish whole.

Ospreys usually build tremendous nests of sticks in the forks of dead trees, but to an Osprey utility poles and even antennas work just as well.

Length: 21 to 25 inches.
Wingspan: 54 to 72 inches.
Habitat: Along saltwater coastlines, freshwater rivers and lakes.
Season: Year round.
Field mark: White head with dark mask, dark above, white underparts, distinctive barred feather markings.

Oystercatcher

The American Oystercatcher is easily recognized by its long red bill and black head as it explores coastal bays and islands where there are oyster reefs. As the name implies, oysters figure prominently in this bird's life. They are experts at opening the small armored mollusks that are exposed at low tide. Using its long wedgelike bill much like an oysterman's knife, the Oystercatcher can open the shell and devour the muscle in the blink of an eye. "Oyster opener" might have been a better name for this bird because oysters don't run very fast! Oystercatchers also eat barnacles, snails, mollusks, crabs and marine worms. A few years ago they were rare, but have once again become numerous and range as far north as New England.

They nest among shells at the high-water mark by scratching out a shallow depression. Eggs are laid in spring or early summer. When threatened, the Oystercatcher will leave the nesting site but the young will instinctively freeze and are so well camouflaged that they are rarely detected. Other names for this bird include oyster bird, clam bird and redbill snipe.

The Oystercatcher does not commonly mix in with other shorebirds, preferring its own company in small flocks. The beautiful yellow eyes and red bill set against the black head make a distinguished-looking bird.

Length: 17 to 21 inches.
Wingspan: 30 to 36 inches.
Habitat: Ocean beaches and mud flats.
Season: Year round.
Field mark: Black head with long reddish orange bill.

Brown Pelican

The clown prince of Florida birds is the Brown Pelican.

Of all the birds that populate the water's edge, the Brown Pelican is without a doubt the most popular seaside attraction in Florida. People have a fondness for this prehistoric-looking bird like no other, and for good reason. Each has its own distinct personality, ranging from whimiscal to adorable, and they are always amusing and playful.

Brown Pelicans prefer the tangled patchwork of mangrove islands for their large nesting colonies. Their nests are 10 to 20 feet above the water and usually 3 to 4 feet apart. The male brings back sticks for the nest and the female usually builds it. Much harmless sparring goes on between neighboring nests. They use their bills to snap at each other, making loud "popping" sounds.

The females lay between 1 and 3 eggs and both parents share the incubation chores. Hatching takes place in 28 to 30 days. Both parents take care of their young and during the 3½ months they are in the nest being raised, they eat over 150 pounds of fish each.

When the seasons change, so do the colors of the pelican's head and neck. Here's a helpful rhyme:

> *Yellow and white*
>   *cool weather in sight*
> *White and brown*
>   *hot weather in town*

The entire population of Brown Pelicans in Louisiana was wiped out in the 1960's by DDT pollution. It had an effect on the egg shells, making them very thin, and most were lost by breakage before they hatched. The chemical worked its way into many food chains, but bird populations are among the first to manifest problems when something goes wrong in the environment. DDT has since been banned and the pelican, state bird of Louisiana, has been reintroduced by restocking from Florida colonies. Now the population is once again thriving.

Pelicans make what looks like controlled crash dives into the water for fish. Just before they enter the water, their wings fold back and the birds torque their bodies sideways. They always surface backwards from where they dive in. Air sacks under the skin of its breast and stomach help take up the impact when they dive. The bill scoops up more than two and a half gallons of water and perhaps a fish or two. Using its muscles, the Pelican squeezes out the water, leaving only the fish to be swallowed.

Many people think there are two different types of Brown Pelicans or that the color differences are male and female, but that is not the case. As with many birds, its color variation depends on the season. There is only one Brown Pelican. In the winter its head becomes a soft yellow with a white "mane" trailing down the back of the neck. In the summer the plumage changes and its head is white and the mane turns a rich brown. These color changes affect both the male and the female. Immature pelicans are an overall brownish color and remain that way up until their third year.

They are excellent fishermen on their own but they find it convenient to sit on pilings where fishermen are nearby to throw them an unwanted fish. During the winter months this habit is sometimes out of necessity when fish move offshore to deeper and warmer water. The Pelicans will do all they can to conserve as much of their energy as possible to the point where they are quite approachable. At times they will even allow humans to pet them. Their feathers are unbelievably soft and the bill can only lightly clamp down on your hand. The worst that could happen is you might get a "paper cut" from the somewhat sharp upper mandible if you pull away too quickly.

Pelicans like sitting on nearby wharfs and pilings waiting for a handout of fish. They are not shy and keep a watchful eye on the human fishermen.

Length: 45 to 54 inches.
Wingspan: Almost 6 feet.
Habitat: Open ocean, bays and wharfs.
Season: Year round.
Field mark: Large dark bill and throat pouch, grayish brown coloring.

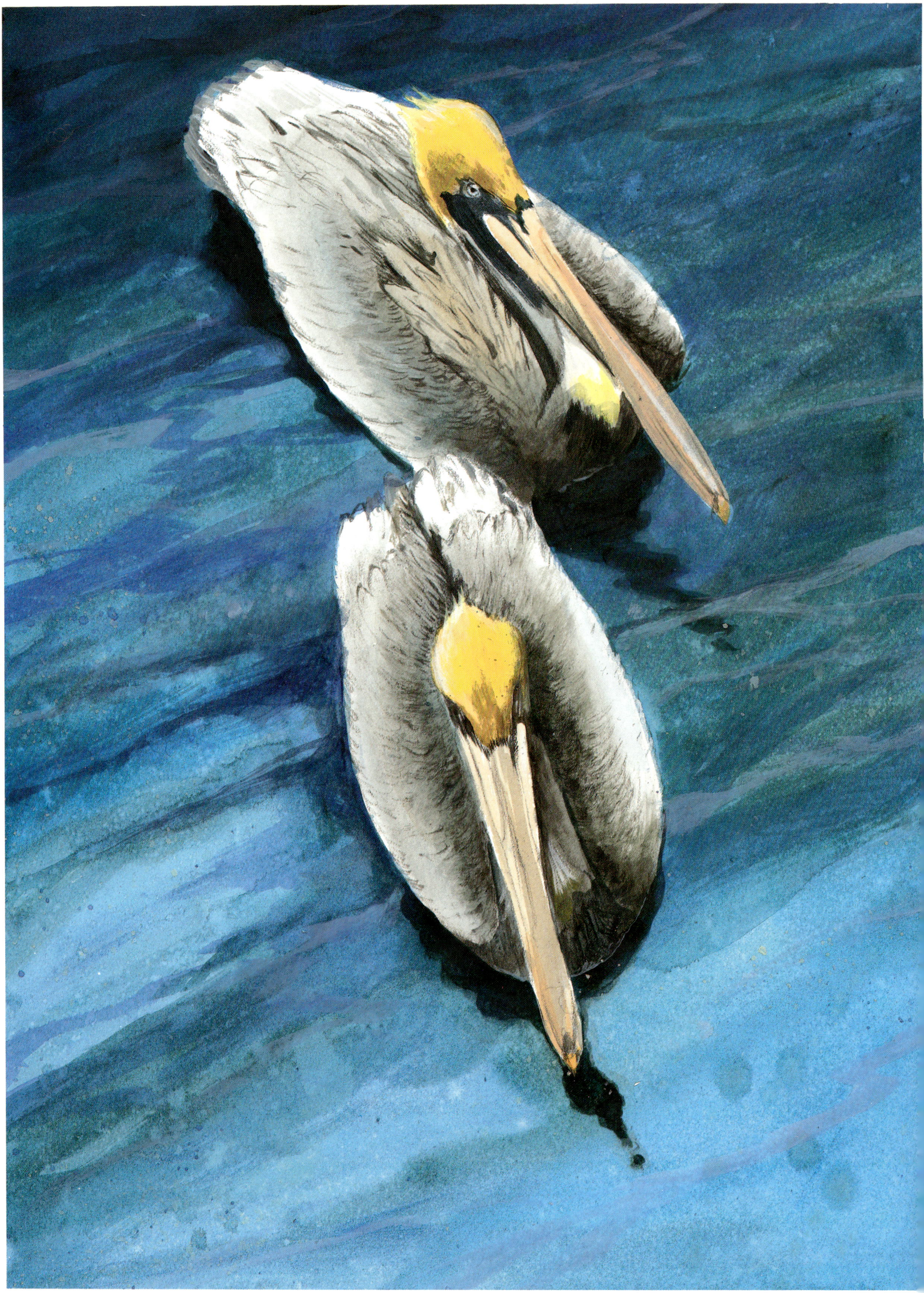

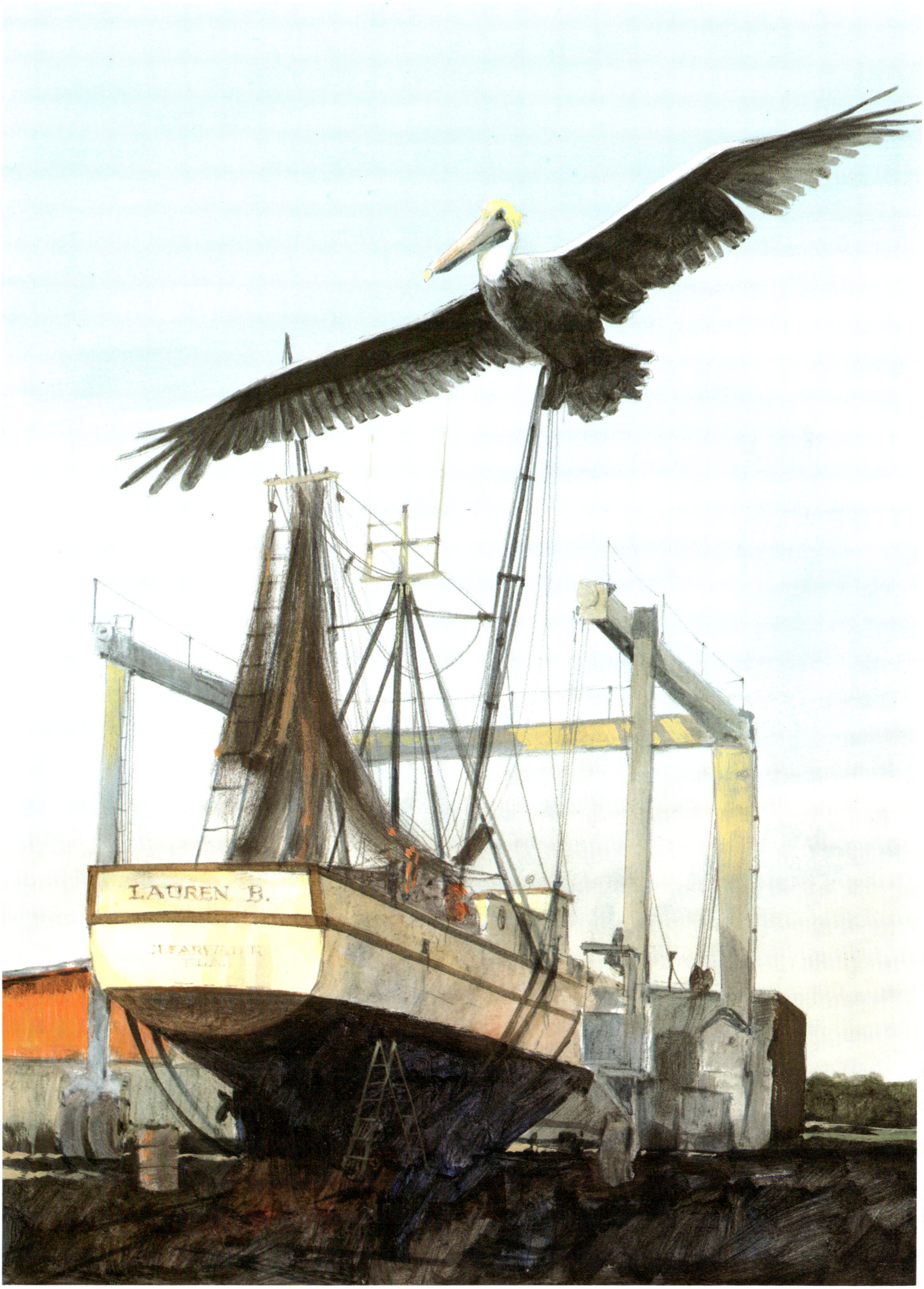
LAUREN B.

White Pelican

Seeing a White Pelican in flight is quite impressive, with its wingspan of nearly nine feet.

Pelicans are often thought of as being Florida birds, but the White Pelican flies in from many northern and midwestern states and from Canada. They stay here during the winter months, although some non-mated birds may stay all year. They are larger than the Brown Pelican and weigh between 10 and 17 pounds, about twice as much as the Brown. The growth on their bill, called a horn, appears during the mating season and gives the White Pelican a strange appearance. No one really knows the reason for this horn. White Pelican nesting areas are crowded and one theory is that the horn helps the young identify its parents, since each horn is a different size and shape.

Their feeding methods are remarkable. Rather than diving for food like the Brown Pelican, White Pelicans work together in large groups on the water, forming offshore in a crescent-shape. Then, almost as if on cue, the birds start to swim shoreward, beating their wings and large webbed feet furiously against the water. As they do this they tighten the arc. This drives the fish into shallow water where the birds use their eighteen-inch-long bills as a dip net. The procedure is repeated until all the birds have their fill.

Length: 54 to 70 inches.
Wingspan: 108 inches.
Habitat: Large bodies of shallow water.
Season: Winter.
Field mark: Very large yellow bill, all white except for black primary feathers.

Sandhill Crane

The Sandhill Crane can be found surveying its inland realm of lakes and fields more often than on the shore. It is one of the largest Florida birds and lives here year round. However, this species is not restricted to Florida and is found as far north as the Arctic. To feed they sometimes stamp on the ground to stir up insects. Foraging for other food is performed by probing with the bill for edible vegetation and invertebrates.

With gray plumage and regal crown, the Sandhill Crane looks the part of a monarch.

A pair of Sandhills will mate for life. During breeding season they break into a spontaneous dance, leaping high into the air with wings slightly spread, followed by courtly bowing to each other. During this season the pebbled skin on the forehead turns a brighter red.

The Sandhill Crane has an unusual characteristic during molting season. Some lose their flight feathers and their ability to fly for a few weeks until new feathers grow in. Cranes fly with their necks outstretched, unlike Herons and Egrets, which fly with their necks drawn back to their shoulders.

A side view of the Sandhill Crane's nostril allows a peculiar view through the bill.

Length: 40 to 48 inches.
Wingspan: 6 to 7 feet.
Habitat: Inland marshlands and prairies.
Season: Year round.
Field mark: Overall gray with red crown.

Shorebirds

Shorebirds is a term used to group together the different species of birds found along salt- and freshwater shorelines and includes Sandpipers, Plovers, Stilts, and Curlews. Most of these amazing little birds nest in the Arctic during the summer months and migrate thousands of miles to Florida and even beyond to South America.

Of all the birds in our book, these birds can be very difficult to identify at first, but the careful observer will enjoy discovering the subtle differences between the species.

Dowitcher

The Dowitcher is easily recognized by its long straight bill and its rhythmic probing in the sand and mud for small marine animals. There are two types, termed Long-billed Dowitcher and Short-billed Dowitcher. They are quite alike except, as you might guess, for the length of their bills. They are about the same body size, but the Long-billed variety is a bit darker in color. As with many other shorebirds, it is a common winter visitor to Florida. Large flocks sometimes number in the thousands.

Length: 11 to 12 inches.
Habitat: Seashore and freshwater marshes.
Season: Winter.
Field mark: Long straight bill, brownish gray over white coloring.

Black-necked Stilt

Striking plumage with the extra long pink legs gives the Stilt an elegant and graceful appearance.

The Black-necked Stilt is abundant in the southwest United States and is seen in Florida primarily along the east coast and the Kissimmee River area. Its long legs give it an advantage over some of its smaller counterparts when searching for small fish and shellfish in deeper water. They can also be a disadvantage in a strong wind, making it difficult for the bird to stand. The Flamingo finds itself in the same situation.

During the mating season they will lay 3 or 4 brown-spotted, buff-colored eggs which have to be turned regularly in the shallow grass-lined or shell-fragment nest. Stilts will courageously defend their nesting site by flying at all intruders, including humans. Insects along with larva and worms are included as part of the Stilt's diet.

Length: 13 to 16 inches.
Habitat: Tidal pools, fresh and brackish shallow water.
Season: Year round.
Field mark: Black and white coloring, very long pinkish red legs.

Willet

The Willet is a large shorebird of the beaches and salt marshes. They live year round in Florida and build their nests on the ground in grassy areas of islands and shorelines. When defending the nest, Willets become quite agitated. Sometimes they will hover, beating their wings excitedly, while at other times their best defense is to sit on the nest motionless and almost invisible.

Repeatedly calling attention to itself with a shrill call of "pilly-will-willet" has quite naturally led to its name. They feed on small marine animals, including crabs, grasshoppers and insects.

Length: 14 to 17 inches.
Habitat: Shorelines and marshes.
Season: Year round, but more numerous in winter.
Field mark: Long legs and bill and light brownish gray coloring.

Yellowlegs

Yellowlegs prefer the calm waters of marshes, ponds and rain pools rather than ocean beaches.

Among the other shorebirds such as Plovers and Sandpipers, Yellowlegs are recognizable by their bright yellow legs and are larger than most other Sandpipers.

They are divided into two species, the Greater and Lesser Yellowlegs. Other than a size difference they are virtually identical. During the winter months, the Yellowlegs can be seen in Florida, although they migrate to the tundra of Canada during the summer. When feeding, the Yellowlegs' bill moves constantly from side to side, probing for small creatures in the muddy bottom.

Lesser Yellowlegs length: 9 to 11 inches.
Greater Yellowlegs length: 13 to 15 inches.
Habitat: Marshlands.
Season: Winter.
Field mark: Dark speckling on white, bright yellow legs.

Long-billed Curlew

This once plentiful species is now a solitary and wary bird. In 1831 Audubon wrote about the Long-billed Curlew, "When we followed them [the Curlews] to the bird banks, which are sandy islands of small extent, the moment they saw us land the congregated flocks, probably amounting to several thousand individuals all standing close together, rose at once, performed a few evolutions in perfect silence, and re-alighted as if with one accord on the extreme margins of the sand bank close to tremendous breakers." By 1920 the Long-billed Curlew had been hunted almost to extinction and even today seeing a Curlew is quite uncommon.

Length: 23 inches.
Wingspan: 36 to 40 inches.
Habitat: Coastal marshlands and beaches.
Season: Winter.
Field mark: Long down-curved bill, brown speckled coloring.

Curlews and Godwits have been identified flying at astonishing altitudes of 20,000 feet.

Whimbrel

When wintering in Florida the Whimbrel lives on coastal beaches and marshlands with other shorebirds. The curved bill is used to penetrate the soft soil, searching for shellfish, worms and marine invertebrates. The Whimbrel will also travel inland to seek out grassy areas for feeding. Whimbrels are attracted to freshly mown golf courses and parks, where they can be seen searching for insects.

Length: 14 to 17 inches.
Habitat: Coastal shorelines and marshlands.
Season: Winter.
Field mark: Down-curved bill, white stripes on head.

Marbled Godwit

The Marbled Godwit is a large North American Shorebird and has a distinctive upturned bill. Its strange name comes from a combination of its coloring and the sound it makes. A rippled pattern of light and dark feathers on its back and neck appear to look much like marble. The Godwit's call is a far-reaching whistle that sounds like "god-wit, god-wit." They probe mud flats for mollusks, crustaceans and worms.

Length: 16 to 18 inches.
Habitat: Coastal beaches and marshlands.
Season: Winter.
Field mark: Upturned bill, brown barred markings.

Black-bellied Plover

The Black-bellied plover inhabits bays and inlets and is larger than most Plovers. It shares the same trait with other Plovers of running on the beach a short distance and then stopping suddenly to feed.

A migratory bird, this Plover is most frequently seen in Florida during the winter, when its plumage is gray and white. In spring, the coloration under the throat and breast becomes a jet black justifying their name black-bellied. They live on a diet of small marine animals including crabs and fish found on the beach. Now and then they will travel to lakes for food.

Although most of these birds nest in the Arctic during the summer, some immature or unmated birds are along our beaches year round appearing rather lonely.

Length: 10 to 13 inches.
Habitat: Coastal beaches and shores.
Season: Winter.
Field mark: Brownish gray with white underparts.

Ruddy Turnstone

This bird really lives up to the title shorebird, as it is rarely seen away from a beach area. Like other shorebirds, the Ruddy Turnstone is migratory and abundant here during the winter. They like to flock together on rocky shores and jetties which have oysters and shellfish. The Turnstone name comes from their habit of turning over pebbles, stones and shells in a diligent search for food.

Length: 8 to 10 inches.
Habitat: Seashore beaches and rocky shores.
Season: Winter.
Field mark: Bright yellow-orange legs, brownish gray with dark throat band over white underparts.

Fishermen have found a surprising tameness about these little birds and they can be seen picking at bait buckets for pieces of shrimp.

Red Knot

Red Knots show an uncommon concern for a single bird should it fall from the flock. The rest will circle back and render what sympathy and aid they can.

Red Knots nest and raise their young in the Arctic. On their migratory route, the Red Knots travel the long distance to the South American coasts. Some birds decide to spend the winter here in Florida and others just pass through during the spring and fall seasons.

Knots travel in large flocks and stop to feed on sandy beaches, mud flats and among rocks. Like other shorebirds, the Red Knot will feed at the surf line. It either picks up marine organisms from a receding wave or by probing for small animals that have buried themselves. When a flock of Red Knots are feeding they appear very impatient. Running and probing for a moment, they will take to the air for a short flight only to land and begin feeding again.

Length: 9 inches.
Habitat: Ocean beaches and shorelines.
Season: Winter.
Field mark: Short bill and gray-speckled back.

Least Sandpiper and Sanderling

As the Least Sandpiper's name implies, it is a small bird often seen alongside other shorebirds running in and out with every wave. The receding waves leave a multitude of tiny marine creatures exposed just long enough for the Sandpipers to pick up their favorite morsel.

Least Sandpipers can also be seen inland on mud flats and lake shores, helping keep the mosquito population down by feeding on larvae.

Least Sandpiper
Length: 5 to 6 inches.
Habitat: Seashore.
Season: Winter.
Field mark: Yellow legs, short bill.

Sanderling
Length: 7 to 8 inches.
Habitat: Seashores, especially sandy beaches.
Season: Winter.
Field mark: Light gray with white underparts, black feet and bill.

The Least Sandpiper and Sanderling both migrate an amazing distance from the Arctic tundra.

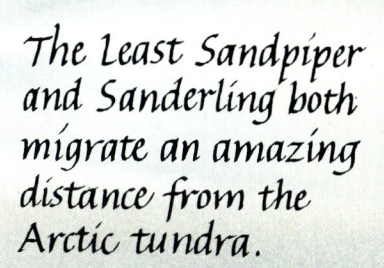

Small and nimble, Sanderlings are among the most common shorebirds and are generally seen in flocks. They also energetically pursue their next meal by following a receding wave, picking up insects and small crabs. They bolt back to shore as a new wave rushes toward them only to repeat the routine over and over. While running on the sand, the legs of the Sanderling move so fast they appear as a blur.

A skittish and nervous little bird, it is difficult to approach. Sanderlings will spring into the air over the least little thing, heading toward the surf and out of harm's way.

Semipalmated Sandpiper

The Semipalmated Sandpiper is a small shorebird seen on Florida's tidal flats and beaches. It can also be found on the shores of rivers and lakes. They live on a diet of aquatic insects taken from soft mud and sandy areas.

This little Sandpiper migrates from its nesting area in northern Canada and appears here in the fall. Most, however, continue to South America. Oddly, the adult Sandpipers begin migration from their northern nesting grounds before their young, leaving them to make the trek on their own. Somehow the young manage to find their way thousands of miles.

Length: 5 to 7 inches.
Habitat: Seashore and mud flats.
Season: Winter.
Field mark: Short black bill and black feet.

The term Semipalmated means "half-webbed," referring to the partial membrane between the toes.

Dowitcher　　Black-necked Stilt　　Willet　　Yellowlegs　　Curlew　　Marbled Godwit

Dunlin

The Dunlin mixes in with other Shorebirds following the advance and retreat of the surf. They prefer ocean beaches and sand bars, but can also be found on inland lakes and rivers.

Dunlins feed in flocks on the beach and take to the air quite suddenly when startled. The closely packed formations move as one while wheeling and turning at high speed and although they are small and plump, they are quick enough to catch insects on the wing.

Dunlins visit our beaches in the winter, migrating from their nesting grounds in the far north. While here in Florida their plumage is grayish and white. You can identify them by their long stout bill that has a distinct downward bend at the tip designed for getting at sand worms. Small shellfish also make up part of their diet.

Length: 7 to 8 inches.
Habitat: Seashores.
Season: Winter.
Field mark: Long, slightly curved bill, grayish color.

Size Comparison of Shorebirds

Black-bellied Plover Ruddy Turnstone Red Knot Least Sandpiper Sanderling Semi-palmated Sandpiper Dunlin

Skimmer

Among Florida birds, the Black Skimmer is one of the most interesting. With its scissorlike bill and black-hooded cape, the Skimmer has a sly look about it.

It is the only bird in the world whose upper bill is shorter than its lower bill, giving it that strange appearance. The bill, which is red with a black tip, is unusually adapted for "skimming" the surface of the water in search of small fish. As the Black Skimmer flies just above the waterline, its lower bill cuts through the surf like a knife. When the long blade touches a fish, its head snaps downward and the upper mandible quickly closes on its prey. Nature has provided strong neck muscles to withstand the sudden impact with its catch.

Skimmers fish anytime but prefer the calm of early evening water when the fish are close to the surface. Their eyes have vertical pupils that narrow to small slits similar to a cat. This helps protect their eyes from bright sand and water during the day, saving them for nocturnal fishing.

During the day Skimmers can usually be seen in flocks gathered together on beaches and sandbars.

Skimmers are a delight to watch as their bills skillfully slice through the water's surface looking for fish.

Sandy shores are favorite nesting sites and can contain several hundred birds. The Skimmer's nest is a shallow depression made of shell fragments. Their eggs are light and speckled, making them practically invisible. In urban areas on the Gulf Coast, the Black Skimmer has tried repeatedly to nest on flat rooftops that have a layer of gravel. While Terns can successfully nest under these conditions, the Skimmer has met with little success. It seems their nests are a little too deep in the gravel, exposing the eggs to the sticky tar and heat underneath.

Length: 18 inches.
Wingspan: 48 inches.
Habitat: Coastal shorelines and bays, some inland lakes.
Season: Year round.
Field mark: Large red-orange bill, black back and white underparts.

Don't be fooled. Skimmers laying in this relaxed position on the beach are only sleeping.

113

Spoonbill

The Roseate Spoonbill with its featherless greenish gray head, pink wings and orange-colored tail qualifies as one of the most stunning Florida wading birds.

In 1930 only 30 Roseate Spoonbills existed in Florida. Plume hunters had all but wiped them out. Today they are still scarce along the shore, but if you keep a sharp lookout among the mangroves you may see them. Usually where one is seen there are others nearby as they are quite social among themselves. When they roost in the dark foliage of the mangroves they are a stunning sight. Although their numbers have increased, their habitats are decreasing. With all the development throughout the south, it is a wonder any exist at all. It would be a shame to lose these special creatures in the name of progress and beach-front condominiums.

The beautiful pink and orange plumage is not the same on every bird and will vary according to the nutrients in their diet.

Spoonbills feed on shrimp, small fish or whatever edible morsel they happen to come across as they anxiously sweep their spoon-shaped bills from side to side. Sensitive nerve endings on the sides of their bills detect any small movement and in an instant their bills snap down around anything they touch. They fly with their necks outstretched like Ibis, Storks and Cranes.

Length: 30 to 32 inches.
Wingspan: 53 inches.
Habitat: Saltwater shallows and mangroves.
Season: Year round.
Field mark: Flattened wide greenish bill and face, mostly pink coloring. Immature spoonbills are all white.

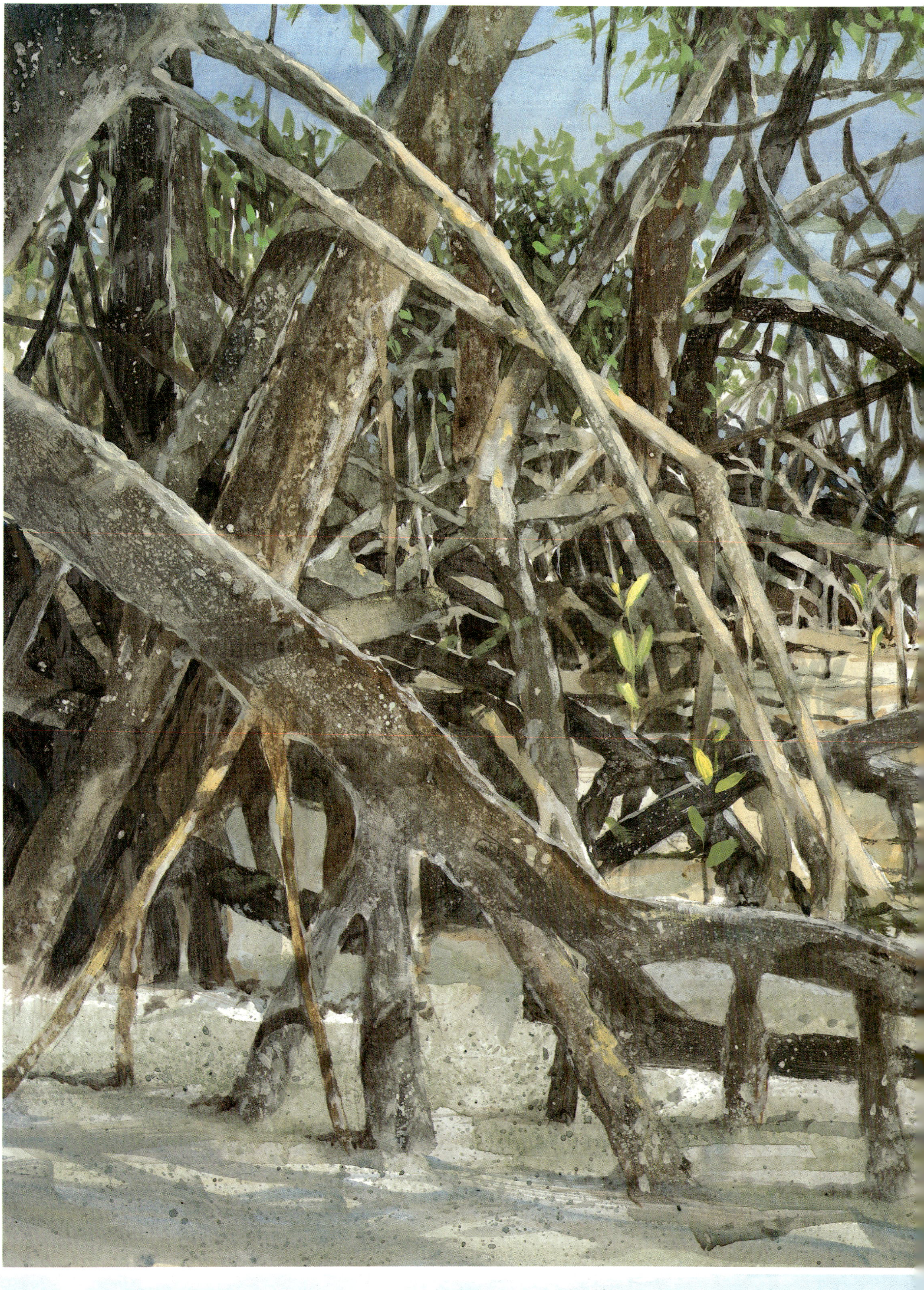

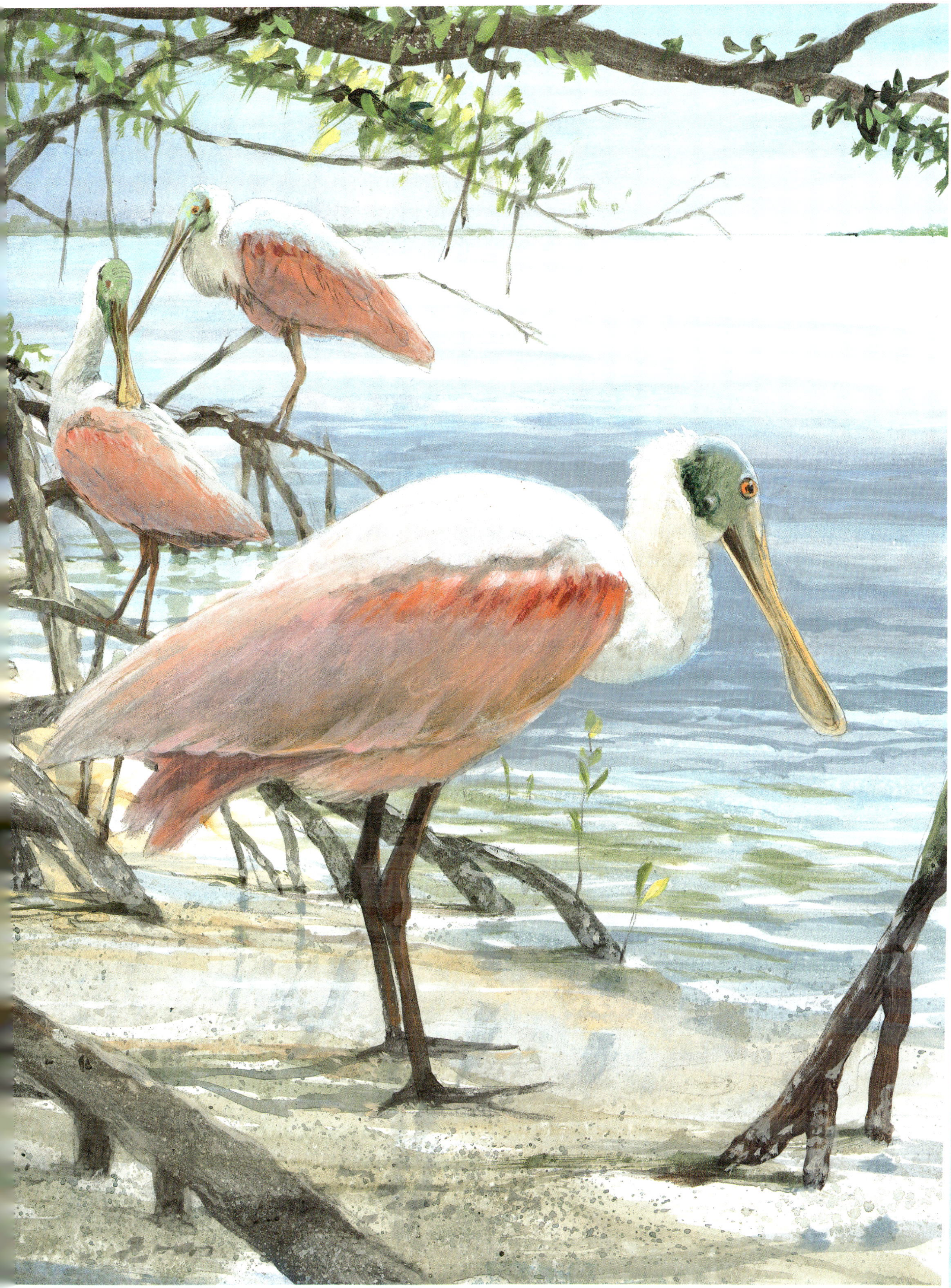

Stork

The Wood Stork brings to mind many childhood stories, but when seen close up, they are anything but romantic looking. The elegant-looking Great Egret might have been a better visual choice to use in illustrated storybooks where new borns were being delivered. The large stick nests they build on rooftops in Europe are, I'm sure, the reason for the fairy tales rather than the appearance of this rather unattractive bird.

This young stork still has feathers on its head. It will lose them when it matures.

It is the only Stork in the United States and is mainly found in Florida. Great colonies of storks nest in cypress trees and mangroves, sometimes dozens in one tree. The nesting begins in November in south Florida and lasts up until May further north. Land development has dramatically disrupted their numbers and 80 percent of the Stork population has disappeared since 1930.

Storks are primarily freshwater feeders, though they do go into tidewaters when the fishing is good. They feed in cooperation with each other, one bird stirring up the water while the others grab the fleeing fish. Like the Spoonbill, Storks also feed by touch, using sensitive receptors on their bill. This ability allows them to feed in muddy water, dense vegetation or at night. When something moving brushes up against their bill a quick response time of only 25 milliseconds, one of the fastest among vertebrates, is all it takes for them to snap their bill shut around the prey. Other names are Wood Ibis and Flinthead.

Length: 40 to 44 inches.
Wingspan: 66 inches.
Habitat: Mangroves and marshlands.
Season: Year round.
Field mark: Large down-curved bill, white feathers except for black flight and tail feathers.

Terns

Sometimes called "sea swallows," Terns have pointed wings, deeply forked tails and display very active aerial habits reminiscent of swallows. There are 42 species of Terns worldwide, seven of which are commonly found in Florida. Terns can easily be mistaken for Gulls, but recognizable differences include the Tern's smaller size, sharper bill and overall streamlined look.

Terns spend a great part of their time in the air, more so than most other birds. They rarely rest on the water as Gulls do and their plumage is only slightly waterproof. Although they plunge/dive for fish, terns do not dive deep or stay in the water longer than is absolutely necessary. They rest on islands, beaches and floating debris but are quite limited when walking or swimming. Their legs are short and feet too weak to aid in catching fish. Instead they rely on their sharp bills to grasp prey.

Nesting in large colonies, Terns choose breeding grounds on remote sandy islands or shorelines having limited accessibility. The colony has a unique defense in the event of bad weather or intruding predators. Young birds unable to fly are formed into a dense group called a "crèche" and are then herded along by adult birds to higher or safer ground. When the danger has passed, adults will locate their offspring by voice recognition, no simple matter in a mob of thousands of Terns all crying as loudly as possible.

Royal Tern

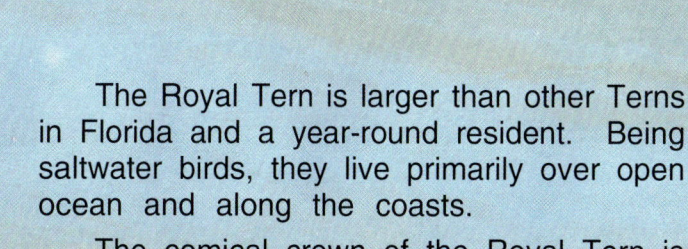

The Royal Tern is larger than other Terns in Florida and a year-round resident. Being saltwater birds, they live primarily over open ocean and along the coasts.

The comical crown of the Royal Tern is made up of elongated black feathers. The forehead is white during the winter and changes to black during the summer months. Their primary diet consists of fish, which they dive on from above, making quite a commotion when they do. Splashing and wing flapping follows as the bird tries again to get airborne.

The Royal Tern scrapes out a nest in the sand and lays one buff-spotted egg then lets the sun do much of the incubation work.

Identifying Terns can be confusing. Since their plumage changes from summer to winter, they are always in some stage of transition, making them even more difficult to distinguish.

Length: 18 to 21 inches.
Wingspan: 43 inches.
Habitat: Seacoast beaches and bays, lakes close to the ocean.
Season: Year round.
Field mark: Orange bill, black crest, forked tail.

Forster's and Common Tern

Forster's Tern
Length: 14 to 16 inches.
Wingspan: 30 inches.
Habitat: Saltwater beaches and bays, lakes close to the ocean.
Season: Year round but more common in winter.
Field mark: Black patch around eye and black bill, forked tail.

Both the Forster's Tern and the Common Tern are the mid-sized species found in Florida. They look very much alike and are light gray on top and white below. In summer both sport black caps.

Terns fly over open water in search of food, often pointing their heads down for a better look below. When a fish is spotted, the Tern will dive headlong into the water.

The diet of these Terns includes small fish, shrimp and almost any kind of flying insect.

Common Tern
Length: 13 to 16 inches.
Wingspan: 31 inches.
Habitat: Saltwater beaches and bays, lakes close to the ocean.
Season: Winter.
Field mark: Black around eye and encircling back of head, forked tail.

Sandwich Tern

Even though the Sandwich Tern may congregate with other Tern species on shore and in the air they do not compete for the same feeding grounds. Most Terns feed close to shore and over inland lakes. But the Sandwich Tern ranges out over deep offshore water, hunting for schools of fish near the surface. They feed in the same manner as other terns by plunging on fish or snatching them with their bills on low passes.

The Sandwich Tern is easy to recognize. The tip of its bill has a small yellow band around it. Just think of it as a spot of "mustard on the sandwich."

Length: 15 inches.
Wingspan: 34 inches.
Habitat: Coastal beaches and open water.
Season: Winter, less common in summer.
Field mark: Black bill with yellow tip, forked tail.

During breeding season, a pair of Sandwich Terns seek a nesting site together usually on an island; in densely populated colonies, competition for the best location is keen. Older adult birds are faithful to their site and return to the same spot every year.

Sandwich Terns are highly sensitive about intruders when in the middle of breeding activity. If the nesting grounds are disturbed at this time, the entire colony may abandon the area.

| Sandwich Tern | Royal Tern | Least Tern | Common Tern | Forster's Tern |

←Winter
←Summer

Brown Noddy and Sooty Tern

Sooty Terns will come ashore for nesting on remote islands, the large colony in North America is on Florida's Dry Tortugas.

Brown Noddy
Length: 15 inches.
Wingspan: 33 inches.
Habitat: Dry Tortugas and open ocean.
Season: Summer.
Field mark: Dark dusky brown with light crown.

Sooty Tern
Length: 16 inches.
Wingspan: 34 inches.
Habitat: Dry Tortugas and open ocean.
Season: Summer.
Field mark: All black above with white underparts, forked tail.

The Brown Noddy and the Sooty Tern share the island area know as the Dry Tortugas, off the Florida Keys. They both search for food in similar fashion, feeding on squid and schooling fish that are close to the surface.

The Brown Noddy does not stray far out to sea. It gets its name from the courting ritual that involves very formal-looking gestures of bowing and nodding to each other.

The Sooty spends most of its time in the air over open water and very seldom lands. It even sleeps while flying. The Sooty Tern will sometimes be blown hundreds of miles away from their breeding colonies by storms and hurricanes, but remarkably they somehow find their way back.

Least Tern

Most birds that winter here in Florida come down from the north. Not so with the Least Tern. It arrives here in the summer and comes up from as far away as Venezuela. As the name suggests, Least Terns are the smallest of the Terns to be seen in Florida. They live along both coasts as well as inland.

The Least Tern feeds on minnow-sized fish and typically searches with head and bill pointed down. When a small fish is spotted, the Tern will hover for an instant and then dive to grab its prey from near the surface.

Least Terns nest in large colonies on sand bars and islands. Eggs are laid directly in the sand without a nest. If an intruder appears, Terns defend their colony with a great ruckus and will even dive on an outsider when threatened.

Length: 8 to 9 inches.
Wingspan: 20 inches.
Habitat: Shallow coastal waters, lakes and rivers.
Season: Summer.
Field mark: Small, black crown, white forehead, yellow bill with black tip.

Vultures

The Turkey Vulture and the Black Vulture are far from being glamorous, but they are good environmentalists. The Vultures are members in good standing with the bird sanitation department, regularly patrolling the roads and countryside for any recent animal fatalities. As scavengers they feed on the carrion of dead or dying animals, helping to clean up what others won't touch.

Turkey Vulture

Sometimes called a buzzard, the Turkey Vulture is the most common. It has a red featherless head and black body. The lack of feathers helps it to keep that part of its body somewhat cleaner and freer of bacteria when eating carrion.

Vultures are experts at soaring and don't need to flap their wings very often as they glide and circle on thermals and upper air currents. On the ground, walking is slow and difficult, so they choose to hop in a heavy ungainly fashion.

Vultures are quiet birds and can only utter weak hissing or grunting sounds. To locate food, it is unclear whether Vultures rely more on sight or smell. General agreement is that Turkey Vultures locate carrion by its odor drifting up on the same thermals on which they soar. However, the Black Vulture seems to rely more on its excellent eyesight to spot food.

Turkey Vulture
Length: 25 to 32 inches.
Wingspan: 6 feet.
Habitat: Marshlands, swamps and prairies.
Season: Year round.
Field mark: Broad two-tone black wings, red head. Very immature has black head.

While flying, the Turkey Vulture's wings are held in a "V" position and can be seen to have two tones of black.

Black Vulture

The Black Vulture's head is grayish and also featherless. Their wings have white patches at the tips that make them easy to identify when in flight.

Both the Turkey and Black Vultures feed mainly on carrion but will occasionally attack defenseless young animals such as newborn calves, piglets and also nesting birds. Even though they are smaller, the more aggressive Black Vultures will intrude on feeding Turkey Vultures and drive them off.

Vultures do not take kindly to interruptions when feeding, and their defense against this is to throw up on any interloper that happens along—which certainly discourages any such intrusion! The slightest scratch from one of these birds is certain to result in infection, so our advice is not to consider one of them as your next pet.

Black Vulture
Length: 22 to 24 inches.
Wingspan: 54 inches.
Habitat: Marshlands, swamps and prairies.
Season: Year round.
Field mark: Broad black wings with white tips, black head.

Final Thoughts

The birds of Florida at the water's edge are among the most magnificent in the world. The colors of their plumage blend with the natural landscape in an unusual camouflage. Shorebirds wear the soft greys and browns of the beaches, other birds are as dark as the tropical vegetation and some are white like the brilliant reflected light on the water. Each species has evolved a specialized niche for itself in our environment and it seems that every opportunity of sustaining life is utilized.

Since my early childhood in Florida, I have been fascinated with the birds around me. To watch and to paint our environment is very rewarding and the genuine thrill of seeing these birds has never grown tiresome for me. I hope our future will provide healthy habitats of undisturbed wetlands for stable bird populations. To prevent the loss of any species requires awareness. What a tragedy it would be to have nothing left except pictures of what once was.

Just outside my door, a freshwater lake sets the stage for daily visits from a pair of Osprey and many Herons, Gallinules and Anhingas. The most wonderful sight is an occasional visit of one or both Bald Eagles from a nearby nesting site. They sometimes fish and once on a quiet Sunday afternoon, they performed their sky dance of courtship. Soaring and wheeling together until they had gained enough altitude, the two Eagles grasped each other's outstretched claws and began to tumble down. As gravity prevailed and they neared the ground, the pair broke apart to begin the ritual once again.

This will always be a lifetime memory for me, but more than that it affirms the wonderment of the bird life around us. We must all remember to protect our environment and to speak on behalf of something that cannot speak for itself.

Bill Renc